Legally Crooked

STOCKMARKET ILLUSIONOLOGY

The art of detecting and analyzing
illusions and deception in the marketplace

**THE ESTABLISHMENT CONTROL SYSTEM
AND ALL ELSE THAT IS DECEIVING**

Anthony Campos, PhD

i

Anthony Campos, PhD

LEGALLY CROOKED

Stock Market Illusionology

First Edition: 2019 revised with new title

Revised from Stock Market Illusionology Edition: 1990

Library of Congress Catalog Card Number: 2012930095
ISBN 978-0-944527-01-6

Legally Crooked
Stock Market Illusionology

By Anthony Campos, PhD

COVER STORY
Walk by faith, not by sight;
Faith is truth but sight may not.
The market eludes like a rainbow in flight,
and the mesmerizing colors exist only in sight.
The illusion of what seems to be an orderly rhyme,
disappears into nothingness after a moment in time.
Anthony Campos

Dedication

Dedicated to Augusto Campos, my father, who advised me from the beginning that the stock market is operated by practitioners of deceit under the guise of public good. I also dedicate this book to Richard Ney whose work inspired me to do further research and development.

A FOREVER BOOK

The operators of all major markets and the operators of the major brokerage houses possess remarkable powers of illusion. They can change lead into gold, and they can change gold into lead all through illusion and deception. This thesis, which is the core of this book, will be valid for as long as there are either multi-facet brokerage houses, non-dependent analysts, market makers or those who possess privileged information. (Anthony Campos)

This presentation is not to be construed as a condemnation. It is meant to be a realization of human nature within the real world where deception can be as legal as a strategy used in a game of poker.

Abuse of Power

It is human nature to desire power.
The attainment of power leads to abuse.
The abuse is then rewarded with greater power.
Greater power is fueled with greater abuse.
The abuse of power will eventually come to light.
Then, human nature dictates a cleansing of conscience.
Once the guilty are subdued, the cycle begins again.
The guilty to be are reborn in a new form of body.

Anthony Campos

x

Table of Contents

INTRODUCTION
1 ILLUSIONOLOGY: The Study of Deception   (1)
2 THE STATE OF BEING LEGALLY CROOKED   (11)
3 THE ESTABLISHMENT CONTROL SYSTEM   (16)
4 THE MARKET MAKER SYSTEM   (23)
5 OPENBOOK CONNECTION   (35)
6 RESEARCH STUDIES   (39)
7 BROKERAGE ANALYSTS   (45)
8 STOCK OPTIONS AND FUTURES   (52)
9 THE FINANCIAL MEDIA   (60)
10 THE WRONG TIME TO BUY   (66)
11 THE DISTRIBUTION STAGE   (68)
12 THE RIGHT TIME TO BUY   (71)
13 THE ACCUMULATION STAGE   (74)
14 WHEN STOCKS ARE MARKED UP   (77)
15 VOLUME AND PRICE   (79)
16 BIG BLOCK ACTIVITY   (81)
17 BLOCK-VOLUME REVERSAL   (85)
18 UPSIDE VOLATILITY   (93)
19 SHORT SELLING ON DECLINES   (95)
20 MARKET MAKER ACTIVITIES & SPECIAL SITUATIONS   (98)
21 SPECULATION   (109)
22 CONTRARIANISM   (114)
23 RULES AND REGULATIONS   (120)
24 TECHNICAL ANALYSIS   (125)
25 ECONOMIC INDICATORS   (135)
26 CRASHES   (140)
27 HISTORICAL EVIDENCE   (144)
28 REQUIRED MENTALITY   (156)
29 PRACTICE ILLUSIONALSYSIS   (159)
CONCLUSION   (164)
REFERENCES   (171)
ADDENDUM   (175)
ABOUT THE AUTHOR

INTRODUCTION

Being deceived without making use of lying is totally legal when erroneous assumptions become the product of he who is deceived. (Anthony Campos)

It shall not be the purpose of this book to change the system however crooked it may be because to do so would completely defeat the true purpose of this work which is to familiarize investors throughout the world about the system. Therefore, the objective is to use this knowledge to make better your investments in the stock market knowing full well that anything that may be considered legally crooked is, in reality, permanently fused into the nature of humanity. For everyone that may accept what is presented here, there will be hundreds that will continue to blindly fuel the legally crooked system of Wall Street and all other world markets. This means that this book will not get outdated nor ever become unusable. While rules, regulations, and laws may change, human nature does not.

The state of being legally crooked, an act of nature, has been in existence since the dawn of civilization. Yet, so many people do not even know what it means, nor do they even realize that it exists all around them. One cannot see the forest for the trees, and so it is that one cannot see the crookedness for the gray of the law. It becomes much like a hidden world that actually exists out of the focus of human vision comparable to the hidden picture within a picture.

When an action is considered legal, it means that the law either allows the action or that there is no law which bars the action. When an action is illegal, it means that a law does bar the action. According to the dictionary, the word crooked is defined as follows: bent; not straight; deformed; dishonest; devious; twisted; tricky; unscrupulous; dishonorable. The definition says nothing about it having to be illegal. Therefore, legally crooked is hereby defined as an action or behavior which may be deemed unethical, immoral or devious, but not addressed by law as being illegal, or if the law is not enforced on a sustained basis.

Thus, the act of being legally crooked represents the philosophy and the act of creating illusions which become the process of deception that is transmitted to the target subject. Therefore, it is the thesis of this work that a stock market and all of its associations represent the biggest and best-coordinated illusion in the world. It can also be argued that the coordination that may be necessary to operate this legally crooked system may actually contribute to a state of efficiency in the markets by the exertion of control.

A system that is legally crooked lacks visibility. The reason why it lacks visibility is that there is a lack of education which produces a widespread lack of knowledge about the system. If the majority of people lack this knowledge, then it means that those who operate the legally crooked system will lend themselves to greed and abuse which may then border on a criminal offense. This has been the situation in the markets and in life throughout all time.

One must realize the limitations of the senses and that all which is physical can be made into a tool of deceit, whether it be through the news media or through a market action. Although it may be difficult to comprehend, the only true reality in the world of financial markets is that which is found in the minds of those in power and in the minds of those who comprehend the human motives of those in power. Furthermore, it must be kept in mind that those in power may represent either the private sector or the public sector.

The true force behind the essence of success can only come from within one's mind. Success can only be lasting if it comes from belief in oneself. Believing in yourself is a prerequisite to the understanding of human motives. Therefore, the study of success in the financial world should be centered on your faith-power and on your understanding of the motivational behavior of those with whom you deal. Of course, whenever your dealings involve money, it should be clearly understood that the one you deal with is, in reality, your opponent.

First, you must recognize your opponents, and then you must realize their motives. Your opponents in the stock market are not other public investors. Instead, your opponents are the exchange insiders who legally have access to nonpublic information and can trade on such information. Thus, the ability to focus is crucial. Operating in the stock market is no different. It is for this reason that the literature in this book extracts those issues that are meaningful out of a conglomeration of static.

Because each of your five senses can be made to perceive something other than what is reality, you must learn to believe in the sixth sense which is your spiritual mind. Whether it is through intuition or visualization, a deceiving situation can only be countered through the free will of the mind. In order to see the illusion for what it is, you must first realize that there must be an illusion. You must develop faith and knowledge from within your own mind. It will be this faith and knowledge that will allow you to possess the courage to acquire contrary positions to the public consensus. It will be this faith and knowledge that will allow you to see the truth that is constantly being masked by the hidden powers of the market.

There are human forces in the market which always seem to be better informed than the public or institutional managers. These forces represent the smart money. The smart money is composed of people who exert their power and influence to attain secret and confidential information concerning economic and corporate decisions. The people involved can be acting in either a legal or illegal capacity depending on their position. Whether the force is from inside or outside the stock exchange establishment makes no difference in the basic method of detection. The key to detecting the direction of the smart money is to place yourself mentally in the position of the smart money, and then consider what you would do to make money by manipulating the majority of all other players outside of your partnership.

The basic concepts of this book can be accepted and used by anyone, whatever his or her beliefs may be. These basic principles can be applied even if the speculator chooses to believe that stocks are not manipulated. Certainly, anyone of reasonable intelligence should accept the concept that stocks go through cyclical periods of accumulation and distribution. Even members of the exchange establishment openly recognize that fact.

Even though the exchange and brokerage establishments clearly believe in the concept of accumulation and distribution as being an acceptable facet of technical analysis, they do not very often mention such analysis in their reports to the public unless it is for purposes of deception.

If there is any argument, it should center on who is doing the accumulation and distribution rather than whether or not these two occurrences really exist. Although methods of detection can vary, volume analysis is standard procedure. Deviation in trading activity is of the utmost importance, whether it be in the shares, in the related stock options, or related to a brokerage house press release.

Price and volume are relative, and there is also relativity between the right players and the wrong players. There is an unseen relativity between many different things in the stock market. This relativity is so well-knit throughout the market that people become apathetic to it all and succumb to the status quo. In general, people are so involved with emotion that they fail to consider how one element may be related to another element. They fail to recognize the motive of the big block seller when prices are high, and they fail to identify the big block buyer when people are forced to sell at low prices. People even fail to notice that volume tends to increase at reversal points.

It is amazing that not much discussion or investigation is ever given to the people who buy or sell at reversal points. While a traditionalist may contend that it is not relevant, a wise person should realize that the short-seller of big blocks at a top or the buyer of big blocks at a bottom must truly be an unusual being to go against the trend.

It is not necessarily a master conspiracy against the public. It most likely is not an organized conspiracy initiated for the sole purpose of fooling the public. Nevertheless, it is a form of natural conspiracy that is built into the stock market system. In other words, the system itself is so designed that it does represent a conspiracy because it gives advantages to those who operate the system. There are no checks and balances. There is no public representation. Even the Securities and Exchange Commission seems to police the public more than the operators of the exchanges. Furthermore, the system represents a conspiracy mostly because the public has never been taught how the market is operated in regards to the opportunities and incentives of working the operation. It becomes an inherent quality of the market that control fosters efficiency, and thus it is acceptable.

The concentration of power does vary in the stock market. During a bull market, it tends to expand beyond the operators of the exchange. However, during a bear market, it contracts to those who are closely linked to the exchange establishment. The reason for this is obvious. There is more incentive during a bull market for outsiders to deal for leveraged takeovers which may tend to exclude exchange members. There are simply more outsiders getting involved with specific issues.

The insider-trading scandals of the 1980s bull market have become fact. These occurrences prove beyond doubt that smart money and manipulation work together. The methods used by these people are in tune with the concepts presented here. The incidents were handled in such a way that investor confidence was not eroded. The SEC and the NYSE succeeded in persuading investors that the system stood for the public good because of the "get tough" speeches presented in the news media. Of course, it was all just propaganda which focused the blame on people other than exchange members.

There has been no difference in market patterns since those trials. People are still being fooled into buying at tops and selling at bottoms. It makes no difference whether the insider-trading is legal or illegal. Why should legal insider-trading produce any different results? The motive is always the same, which is to get stock cheap and sell it at a higher price.

Early into the new century, we had the federal charges against the NYSE specialists which came about only because the abuse became so apparent it could not be hidden by any illusion. However, once again, it became merely a show by the government resulting in monetary fines. Agreements were made so that the major forms of illegalities would be buried for fear that it would show a totally corrupt market system.

Immorality and unethical behavior do evolve into more serious stages over a certain period of time. The specialists of the NYSE operated for decades without challenge. This means that for decades the crookedness evolved to the point that the process crossed the line into something illegal by law. However, by definition, crookedness does not have to be illegal by law, and so we can wonder about how much crookedness remains in process that is not addressed by law.

Legal insider-trading by exchange operators in collusion with corporate insiders is the most damaging to the public because it makes use of all the elements in the system. In other words, it is more efficient and widespread, and therefore, it involves much more money. Indeed, a system that lacks ethics and morality can actually become very efficient.

Market cycles work well for the exchanges because a bear market tends to concentrate the power back to those who operate the market. This is true because outsiders either go bankrupt or find less incentive in the market. Whatever the case, a good bear market does serve the purpose of bringing power back to those who operate the exchange system. An erosion of wealth occurs amongst the public. Gone with wealth is power. In other words, the exchange insiders that are short the market will drain capital from the public investors.

People who oppose this philosophy will always respond by saying that it is paranoia to believe that manipulation exists in the market. However, they always fail to offer evidence to refute this viewpoint of the stock market system despite all of the evidence. Meanwhile, these same people will agree that insider knowledge is shared by market makers and other brokerage authorities. Is it therefore not true that manipulation stems from insider knowledge?

Whenever possible, credible sources are entered as references so that the reader knows this is a work of research. This work proceeds from the presentation of evidence to logical conclusions. The evidence is sporadically widespread, but it is hidden within the forest of informational leaves. The purpose of this book is to spotlight those leaves within the forest that make light of what is really important. In the end, the reader determines the verdict on whether or not the control establishment is legally crooked.

Tribute to Richard Ney: by the author, Anthony Campos

I began to follow Richard Ney in 1982 when I founded The Wall Street Inquirer. I received Ney's newsletters and phone messages over the years. Whenever I wrote to him, he responded. I learned the basic system from him, and then I began to do my own research. In 1990, I self-published "Stock Market Illusionology" based on my beliefs which were in accord with Richard Ney. Therefore, "Legally Crooked" represents an easy to read and an understandable composite of stock specialist analysis carried forward into other financial entities that have taken over the power structure of the specialist system. The basics remain the same; only the sophistication has changed to a much higher level.

When Richard Ney passed away on July 18, 2004, I was glad to know that he got to see the start of the fall of the specialist empire. What he had preached, and what the media had denied, finally came to light. However, it is my opinion that Richard Ney has not been fully recognized for his work and has not received retribution for the arrows shot at him by the establishment and the financial media. While he may not have written his fourth book before his death, I decided to continue the philosophy of his basic principles and to reflect all that has occurred since. I write "Legally Crooked" without fear and with the full confidence that I bring forth my own ideas backed up with research that will tend to reinforce Richard Ney's basic philosophy by covering issues other than the stock specialist system. While Ney tended to rightfully concentrate on the specialist system, I will concentrate on the crooked system of the brokerage establishment that takes the place of the fallen specialist empire.

Anthony Campos

1

ILLUSIONOLOGY: The Study of Deception

Illusionology is hereby introduced as a valid branch of learning. This term was introduced in an earlier form of this work in 1990 under the title of "Stock Market Illusionology." This is the study and understanding of illusions or perception concepts. In a more specific form, stock market illusionology is the art of detecting and analyzing illusions and deceptions in the marketplace, while illusionalysis, which was also coined in the same book, is simply the process of detecting illusions, or that which may not be readily visible, and determining meaning and course of action to be taken. All of the stock markets throughout the world can be considered under this guidance. The central definition is that illusionology is the study of deception.

An illusion may come in many forms. Its composition can vary on a spectrum from physical to psychological. However, its perception is almost entirely psychological or emotional. For example, a ten-acre dump can be covered and landscaped to look beautiful. On the surface, this situation has become a physical illusion of a great place to live. On the other hand, a psychological illusion is when a person absorbs information from the media and is influenced into making a wrong decision. Either way, the senses transmit the illusionary image to the brain where it becomes a psychological process of perception.

Illusions are constantly being fabricated in the market. While sometimes their existence is built into the system, illusions are quite often created by those who stand to profit from those who perceive the illusion as real. While there may be several entities responsible for springing illusions upon the public, it is the market makers and other inside operators that are true masters of the art of illusion in the market. Of course, upon releasing economic data and reports, the government can also participate in creating illusions which may benefit those in federal power and which may benefit those in the marketplace that comprehend the illusion.

The results of illusions are almost always of mutual benefit to all exchange insiders because these people are all connected to each other much like a nerve system. It can be thought of as being a transfer of information by pulse between the members. It is simply an extraordinary form of teamwork.

An investor must recognize the possibility of an illusion at or near a turning point. The media becomes the tool of choice. The main prerequisites for being able to realize the truth about propaganda are the following:

1. Always be suspicious of the general consensus.
2. Always be skeptical of experts being presented in the media.
3. Always consider the financial motivations of others.
4. Always consider contrary thinking.
5. Always question how a bottom line number was originated.
6. Always observe how words are used within a news release.

Once the possibility has been established that an illusion is being created to fool investors, one must then relate the situation with the course of stock prices and news static. At this point, one must consider the following:

1. the most valid of your indicators
2. big block activity in the major stocks
3. place more importance on technical analysis
4. make no decision to commit if in doubt
5. apply contrary thinking to your analysis
6. play the part of a market maker
7. always consider "what if"

Like magicians, stock specialists (market makers in general) are masters of illusion. They can control price movement enough to give investors the wrong impression about the future. For the most part, specialists and those associated with exchange insiders are at the core of initiating deceit. Illusions can also be considered built into the stock market system. In other words, illusions are often unknowingly propagated by news media people and analysts who are so grossly wrong about the market that exchange insiders need only sit back and enjoy the show. Brokerage analysts set the mood, and then outside analysts form conclusions. When these are put together, the news media initiates a financial headline.

One must always expect an illusion to be propagated by a seller or buyer. The only thing in question is the quality or sophistication of the illusion. A seller will upgrade the product to present a myriad of good fortune, and of course, a buyer will downgrade the product to present a picture of despair.

The physical senses are especially subject to illusion whenever the sixth sense of spirit-mind and faith is lacking. In other words, one must be in mental possession of a code of behavior. The power of this code of behavior should be drawn from a book of faith such as a religious bible, etc. It can also be drawn from experience in life dealing with the real-world motivational behavior of people. Once a standard has been established, one can then develop an individualized code of financial behavior. The following is just an example.

1. Never accept pat answers as gospel.
2. Think for yourself; follow your code.
3. Do not be a trend follower after a prolonged move.
4. Question that which feels obvious.
5. Control fear and greed.
6. Never be embarrassed to question.
7. Realize that intimidation is to benefit the intimidator and is used to reinforce his illusionary deception.

In order for an illusion to succeed, the one creating the illusion must have his subject concentrate on something which does not give away the process. When the market forms a top, the investor must be made to see strength and not the underlying weakness. The opposite is true when the market is forming a bottom.

Of course, it is a well-known fact that not many people know about the elements of accumulation and distribution. There are not even many private analysts who operate sophisticated systems of detecting cash in-flow and out-flow. Whatever the case may be, the average investor can train himself or herself to recognize illusions by applying the principles found herein and learning to interpret chart patterns and volume figures. Learning how the market maker works and thinks like an agent of a higher power should be your primary concern, and this is what this literature concentrates upon.

Also, for an illusion to succeed, the targeted subject must be influenced by some sort of excitement. In other words, the physical senses have to be activated in order to keep the targeted subject from questioning what is being witnessed. In reality, an illusion is merely a deception or misimpression.

An example of an illusion can be cited that was perpetrated by a real estate broker upon a visitor to Idaho from another state. The visitor went to see a parcel of land out in the country. It was a typical country scene with cow pastures surrounding the area. There was also an unfinished house next door. It was a very large house with expensive looks. When the broker was asked about the house, he said that the owner was building it a little at a time. He implied that such a house next door would increase the value of those properties around it. Needless to say, the visiting prospect had visions of building a house on the parcel of land next door to this grand structure that was being erected.

It was quiet. The grass was green, and the flowers were sprouting all around the five-acre lot. The birds were all chirping in a happy fashion, and the cows in the pasture next door were a picture of contentment. Everything was peaceful.

He bought the parcel accepting that nothing was wrong since the broker gave no warning of anything being wrong. The visitor accepted the broker as a servant of mutual benefits of all concerned. The visitor went back to his home state believing that he had a good deal. He now had a large piece of land on which he could now build his future home.

It was several months later that a relative of this man sent him a newspaper clipping from the area. There it was, a full picture of the unfinished house with his property in the background. His future neighborhood was making the news. Unfortunately, the unfinished house was being condemned by the local county. According to the paper, the house was sinking, and toxic gas was leaking up through the ground. That seemingly serene and beautiful country setting was the location of a deep crevice filled over time by garbage. It was hard to believe that the noise of trucks and the smell of filth once reigned supreme in that place. With the whole state to choose from in all its beauty and splendor, he had bought himself a dumpsite. The dumpsite was not disclosed by the broker.

The motivation to make money is not easily countered by integrity or conscience. The buyer that got fooled should have made neighborly connections, and he should have relied upon his own investigation. However, it becomes part of human nature to entrust our souls to those that possess a government-issued license.

Perhaps the most well-known illusion in the market is when the market is giving the impression of strength while the advance-decline line is going lower. Although this is an example of a market illusion, it really is a very low-level type of illusion. In this example, when the euphoria of an advance is in process, most investors may not be inclined to observe for anything negative.

A much higher level of illusion in the market is when market makers are either unloading or shorting stock onto investors based on good news or accumulating stock from investors based on bad news. Can these actions be considered immoral and unethical? Yes, they can. Can these actions be considered illegal? No, they cannot. When it comes to finance and investments, there always seems to be a great area of grayness in the law. That gray area is where things are considered legally crooked.

There have been many cases where the illusion is one of impending inflation while in reality disinflation exists. The media is often used to help create the illusion by releasing either false or misleading information. When the media is involved, the illusion of economic strength or weakness is sure to succeed, because the public tends to accept the American journalist as being dedicated, moral and truthful.

It all depends on the conditioning of the mind. The figure which is shown here does illustrate the concept very well. What exactly do you see in the image which is presented? If you are conditioned to receive the image of an old woman, you will see exactly that. On the other hand, if you are conditioned to receive the image of a young woman, then you would see that image immediately upon looking at the picture. Both images are present at the same time, but the viewer will initially only see one of them.

Ambiguous picture of a young woman and an old woman. (*Source: Edwin G. Boring, "A New Ambiguous Figure," American Journal of Psychology, July 1930, p. 444. Also see Robert Leeper, "A Study of a Neglected Portion of the Field of Learning—The Development of Sensory Organization," Journal of Genetic Psychology, March 1935, p. 62. Originally drawn by cartoonist W. E. Hill and published in Puck, November 6, 1915.)*

The news media is capable of employing hypnotic writing into the headline and into the body of an article to accomplish the effect of conditioning the reader into performing in any particular manner. As a result, a bearish situation can become bullish simply by suggestion through the use of keywords. In other words, gold can be turned into lead, and lead can be turned into gold in a very short period of time.

In the financial world, an investor can be conditioned to perceive only what the deceiver wants him to see. The conditioning is often accomplished through reinforcement. In other words, there is a bombardment of input to the investor which tends to emphasize a central idea or a slanting in a specific direction such as making a big profit. This can be done so powerfully through the media that an investor will block all the factors which are contrary to the projected image of the deceiving element. It is a fact of life that the public is highly impacted by the media.

When exchange insiders and other associated parties want to accumulate stock, they will create an illusion of an overheating economy which will lead to greater inflation which will lead to higher interest rates. This illusion will be accomplished through the media with the release and emphasis of certain economic figures accompanied by the appropriate commentary. While this is occurring, there will be no emphasis on the fact that gold is going lower, that money supply is easing, that most of the commodities are in a downtrend and that the economic figures being released may not even be accurate. Under these conditions, the investor will see the illusion of a very weak market and sell his stock, or even worse he may sell short.

An illusion can be considered a form of perception that distorts reality. It is a general impression not consistent with the true situation. For example, the following images look proper, and most people would say that the images represent something realistic. However, upon careful inspection of the parts, it becomes apparent that these images are not consistent with reality. (These are open source images taken from the Internet.)

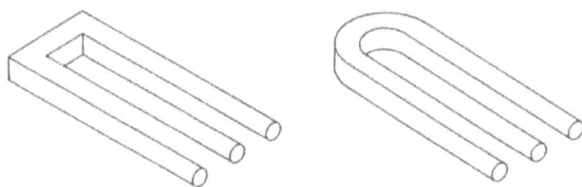

In order to recognize a deceitful situation, it is a good idea to observe some of the individual components. In other words, the deceiving image represents the sum total (e.g., Dow Industrial Average), and so it becomes important to look at the component parts of the Dow Industrials. If brokerage associated analysts try to paint an image of a major market top, and if you notice that several of the major Dow stocks have not reached distribution levels, you can be reasonably sure that the market will not crash but will most likely go higher. This can also be applied in reverse when the market is in a bearish phase.

The thesis which has been presented in this work is that exchange operators create illusions to influence investors to behave in a controlled manner. It is important that one recognize this so as not to misread the true situation and make similar misjudgments that "influenced" investors are likely to make. Therefore, contrary thinking is the key that unlocks illusionary perception to reality. The objective of contrary thinking is to invest as exchange insiders are investing.

The investor must realize that the news media is not going to give the solution to acquiring wealth. Otherwise, everyone would become wealthy, and of course, this has never happened in history. There is not enough money in the system. Therefore, there must be a transfer of capital to a select few that most likely operate with unique methods, unlike the general public.

The illusions created in the marketplace can be of different types. For example, one situation can be that market makers want investors to see a positive market instead of a negative one. This scenario would be much like the young lady/old lady illusion. Another situation may be that market makers are highlighting a stock to the public for the purpose of distribution

8

while camouflaging obvious flaws in the company's operations. This scenario would be much like the unrealistic illusions of the forks. Still another situation could very well be that a company which is in good shape and prime for investing is portrayed and distorted as a problem in order to get investors to sell as market makers accumulate.

This scenario would be much like the following two examples where the objects are in perfect shape (a perfect square and a perfect circle) but are portrayed as being troubled by distortions. While these distortions may be graphic in nature, it is possible that words, photographic scenes, and passages in a document can be so designed to deceive the eye and still be considered legal under the law. (open source images from the Internet)

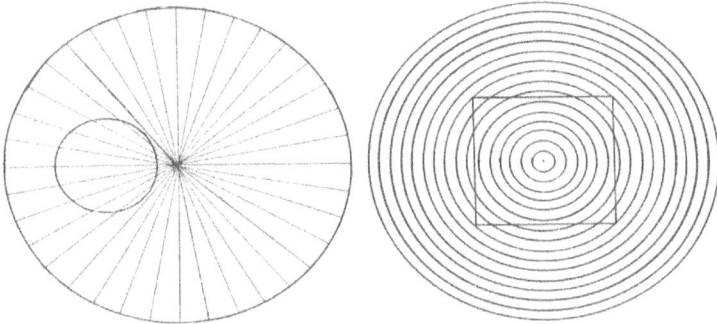

the inner circle is perfect; but looks distorted / the square is perfect; but looks distorted

A very common type of illusion or deception that may be employed by the media is manifested by the headline of either a news article or press release. For example, if a company report contains both positive and negative news, and if the control establishment wishes to emphasize the negative news, then the writer of the article will present certain key words into the headline that will emphasize the negative angle. While the positive news may still appear within the article, it will be the headline that will register on the minds of the reader. It will be the headline that will appear by itself within all the links on the Internet. In other words, the headline governs the body of the written article.

The following statement by Christ, taken from the Bible, is a fine example of the virtues of contrary thinking. "Go in through the narrow gate, because the gate to hell is wide and the road that leads to it is easy, and there are many who travel it. But the gate to life is narrow and the way that leads to it is hard, and there are few people who find it." (Today's English Version - Matthew 7:13-14)

There are many wide gateways to the financial markets. However, the gateway that leads to success is narrow, and it is hidden by illusions which have been constructed, not by nature, but by those who have a license to operate the gateway. This system of financial illusions is not restricted to one nation. It is worldwide. The richest market operators in the world continue to do well because they have connections to sources not available to the general public. While the law allows this privilege to be legal, it is certainly crooked.

2

THE STATE OF BEING
LEGALLY CROOKED

The state of being legally crooked is an act of nature that has been in existence since the dawn of civilization. It is amazing that so many people do not know what it means, nor do they even realize that it exists all around them. It can be described or defined as a hidden world that exists out of the focus of human vision. Furthermore, this state of being legally crooked is very closely associated with the art of illusionary deception. These two elements become supported and strengthened in transmission by the highest attainable levels of efficiency. Therefore, the state of being legally crooked can exist at its highest level of force when supported by illusionary deception with a resulting high level of perceived efficiency.

A good example of this process goes back to the specialist system at the NYSE. The specialists found ways to bend the rules by deception, but they presented an atmosphere of efficiency by keeping the market orderly. As long as they kept the market orderly with operational efficiency, the specialists were able to either bend the rules or perhaps commit unethical practices. It shall be the thesis of this book that the process of being legally crooked continues to evolve to a much higher level of existence.

The following is a reiteration of the definition found in the introduction of this work. When an action is considered legal, it means that the law either allows the action or that there is no law which bars the action. When an action is illegal, it means that a law does bar the action. According to the dictionary, the word "crooked" is defined as follows: bent; not straight; deformed; dishonest; devious; twisted; tricky; unscrupulous; dishonorable. The definition says nothing about it having to be illegal. Therefore, legally crooked is hereby defined as an action or behavior which may be deemed unethical, immoral or devious, but not addressed by law as being illegal, or if the law is vague or questionable or not enforced on a sustained basis.

The state of being legally crooked is deception. Deception does not have to be illegal. In playing a sport or a game, it is legal to deceive. Being deceived without the use of lying or breaking a law is totally legal when assumptions become the product of he who is deceived.

Robert W. McGee (2007), who holds several doctorate degrees, states in one of his many scholarly articles that what is unethical may not be illegal. This tends to corroborate the definition of legally crooked since an unethical act tends to mean crookedness in behavior. McGee goes on to imply that certain types of insider trading may actually be beneficial to the investment community which tends to validate that perceived efficiency may be the result.

However, McGee considers insider trading to be the illegal kind by law involving people other than market makers. On the other hand, it is my contention that insider trading includes market makers and all of the management of investment brokerage houses. By law or lack of law, brokerage market makers can trade on inside information for the purpose of maintaining an orderly or efficient market. It is for that reason that I classify market makers as being legally crooked, but I also give them credit for maintaining a fair degree of efficiency in the markets. Nevertheless, it is contended here that the produced efficiency is for the purpose of maintaining the illusion of the perception of efficiency for the purpose of self-profit.

At this point, the reader must understand that inside information may not be as clear as may be assumed by the law. If an individual makes an out of the ordinary transaction, it will show up in a pronounced manner. If shortly thereafter, major news is released concerning that issue, a regulatory entity of the government will target that transaction. However, since a market maker initiates so many transactions in the course of several days, it becomes very difficult to prove that either a market maker or anyone associated with a major brokerage firm is guilty of any wrongdoing. For this covert activity to succeed on a continual basis, those who have inside information must never pass that information to an individual outside of the company perimeter. In other words, it becomes a strict connection between the market maker supervisor and the company analyst. If the analyst is the collecting source, then it becomes his or her job to obtain information using whatever loopholes may be available. The people that work for a brokerage firm or have a license are well-trained in regulatory procedures. They know how to operate at the edge of the law and remain legal.

H.G. Manne (1966), a reputable author of many scholarly journal articles and books, defined insider trading as any form of trading based on information that is relevant for the fundamental value of a company that is not publicly available. If Manne's definition is accepted, then it would mean that market makers may at some point become inside traders by definition. As can easily be realized, this may lead to confusion. However, it is this confusion in the law that allows market makers to know material nonpublic information that allows them to trade for the brokerage in order to maintain market efficiency and liquidity.

There has been a marked contrast between the Nasdaq dealers and the traditional specialist system of the NYSE. However, the tendency is moving in the direction of fusion. In other words, the specialist partnership firms are being absorbed by the major brokerage establishments. When this process is completed, it will mean total domination by the investment bank establishments. There are certain critical implications derived from this process of fusion which can only lead to the advantage of the establishment control system.

The specialist units either are or were small compared to the big brokerage houses and were easier to investigate because of their smaller operational size. The big brokerage houses, on the other hand, are widespread conglomerates with many operational departments in which incoming revenue can be categorized or masked into many various avenues. Not even the Internal Revenue System nor any Congressional agency may fully comprehend the thousands of inflow and outflow trails of capital movement. The sophistication of operational procedures of the brokerage establishment may well dwarf that of the government.

Further clarification may be required on the matter concerning perceived efficiency and liquidity. The research writers mentioned here are using the term "efficiency" to mean a strictly defined situation which is supposedly positive for the public good by supplying liquidity. The reader should note that I used the term "perceived efficiency" to mean that market makers, as inside traders, may at times merely present the appearance of being efficient in serving the public investor.

According to Peter-Jan Engelen and Luc Van Liedekerke (2007), there are different types of insider trading where insider trading may produce efficiency or when nonpublic information may be used for manipulation, in which case it would decrease market efficiency. In other words, manipulation will create inefficiency by moving the price away from a true valuation. This inefficiency comes about when a market maker purposely either lowers or raises the price by exerting trading operations on a particular issue.

It is contended here that market makers may demonstrate both types of insider trading qualities. While the market maker may employ true efficiency, the subject individual may also employ manipulation which may not lead to market efficiency but may be perceived as efficient, or the occurrence will most likely not be noticed at all. It has already been introduced here that an act of deception which is really based on manipulation is meant to be covert.

Levels of Being Legally Crooked

It is proposed here that the act of being legally crooked can be broken into degrees of intensity. For the purpose of demonstrating the intensity of an event, we shall use the following designations of 1st degree, 2nd degree, and 3rd degree. This means that a first-degree offense is more serious than a third-degree infraction.

1st Degree

Written rules, regulations, laws and/or policies are violated but not enforced. Laws may be circumvented with questionable loopholes, causing financial or social damage to a party. In other words, quite often a law can be broken or bent, but not enforced by the regulatory agency due to a loophole that may not be addressed by the law. It may also become that a regulatory agency may simply not enforce the law.

2nd Degree

This may be considered a gray area of the law. It is premeditated deception and/or manipulation not covered by a law. The event is considered unethical, causing financial or social damage to a party. Thus, an act can be considered unethical, but still considered legal if not addressed directly by law. In other words, an illegal action cannot occur unless there is a law that may address the action, or be that some form of link in the law can be associated with the action. In those cases where there may be grayness in the law, it becomes the opinion of a Supreme Court to judge the case.

3rd Degree

This may be considered completely legal but still unethical by virtue of intent. It is deception, accompanied with manipulation, based on usage of definitions and meanings of words and/or actions with selected elements omitted, causing obstruction of a full and valid analysis of an event which may or may not lead to financial or social damage to a party. The emphasis of this level rests on the theory that public opinion may be diverted by covert means in a particular direction with intent to deceive. This category may include economic reports, press releases, news media releases, brokerage upgrades, and downgrades, etc. This level of being legally crooked is the most common event throughout the market. It has become common practice.

3

THE ESTABLISHMENT CONTROL SYSTEM: MANIPULATION

Smart money represents the people who are investing correctly in the market. There is general agreement on this portion of the definition; however, the controversy deals with the following question: Do the smart money people possess manipulative power?

While most people believe that the smart money group is a constantly changing group of individuals, the power of common sense, logic, and reasoning behind the present literature believes that the opposite is true. Therefore, the full definition as accepted herein is as follows: *Smart money* is that element in the financial world that knows critical information not known by the public and is in the position of investing huge amounts of money according to such privy information. As a result, this smart money faction is able to exploit the weaknesses of the mutual funds sector. In other words, smart money is not just people who are right on account of luck or because of their intelligence.

The establishment control system is composed of many facets of which all are connected. The big brokerage houses have become connected with major capital markets by either being owned by major banks or because they own major banks. It becomes such a tight fusion between brokerage houses and banks that it becomes entirely acceptable to consider such partnerships as investment banks.

Manipulation is control. Control used to be under the domain of the NYSE, but certain events have changed this. Power has gone to a higher level of sophistication. However, the process remains the same. In one of his three books "Making It in the Market," Richard Ney eloquently explains the process for which the NYSE can now be replaced by the investment banking establishment.

The public's carefully engineered images of the investment process are rooted in its assumptions about the integrity of its political, financial, and media institutions. Lacking legitimate insights into the motivations of those who head these institutions, investors are unaware that, as aspects of the investment process, they too are controlled by the big-money forces that dominate the insider establishment of the major exchanges.

According to Ney (1975), an investor should not attribute losses to either economic circumstances or his incompetence. Instead, the blame should fall upon the magician's hand which is not being observed or studied. In other words, investment losses are due to an education system that turns people into puppets by exerting the philosophy that crookedness cannot ever be defined as being legal. Furthermore, the education system fails to educate the people that the media may become an arm of those financial institutions that may have a conflicting interest in the financial markets.

The objective of manipulation is usually to develop marketability in a stock so that the manipulator will be able to dispose of large amounts of it when he desires to do so. In other words, he tries to create a broad market on which to sell. At this point, it is appropriate to say that manipulation is synonymous with the establishment control system, which is to say that it is associated with the big brokerage houses, brokerage analysts, brokerage dealers and any media entity that is financially tied to any investment establishment. Therefore, the manipulative system of the major brokerage houses is very extensive. The power of the brokerage establishment must not be underestimated. It is a power that supersedes that of the stock specialist.

Let us regard manipulation as being related to the following: (1) It is used in the marking-up or marking-down stage of a market movement. (2) It is done for the purpose of enticing the public to buy when the operator wishes to sell and to sell when the operator wants to accumulate. (3) It is used to decrease or increase activity in a stock in order to prepare the way for the operator to accomplish his goals. Each market movement, whether

17

short-term or long-term, has three stages. A bullish operation would entail the following: (1) accumulation, (2) marking-up, and (3) distribution. A bearish operation would involve the following: (1) distribution or short-selling, (2) marking-down, and (3) covering short positions. These are the same principles that drove the success of John R. Keene who was perhaps one of the greatest manipulators of the late 1800s.

It is very important that the speculator form an opinion as to which of these stages a stock is going through. The trader must learn to sense the trend of the movement if he or she is to be in tune with the operator or other smart money element.

It is amazing that, as far as the public is concerned, the commercial rule of thumb, which makes a product less desirable the higher its price, is totally reversed in the market. The higher a stock goes the more interest is aroused amidst the public. In other words, those who have a profit believe they will get more, and those not holding the stock become more anxious to get a share of the action.

Instead of slowly letting go at a price that shows a good profit, the average trader will want to buy more and more and find himself with his largest load at the top. This kind of buying is often instigated by a sustained upward movement. Needless to say, this type of sustained movement is very convincing and creates buyers in proportion to the urgency shown by the price movement (get it before it's too late). This type of public behavior leads us to a basic concept. The smart money or brokerage traders do the opposite of what the public is undertaking after a prolonged upward movement.

Although the NYSE specialists or the NASDAQ dealers are the main smart money agents of the control establishment complex, they are not the only type of smart money. All those exchange insiders who deal with the market makers as clients should also be considered part of the smart money system. The specialist will buy and sell big blocks of stock for exchange insiders (the administrative people of the exchange and their friends), and he will also do business for his special clients including the upper echelon of the brokerage establishment. There is no doubt that the specialist will act as an agent for special clients when dealing in very big blocks of stock. This inside connection to the big money sources is what gives the specialist more power than what most people realize. As a result, the specialist has an enormous pool of capital from which to draw upon at reversal points. He has not only his own capital but also that of others. He uses the money of others to fully employ his power. Keep in mind that many of the major brokerage houses are presently owned by major banks.

It must be emphasized that the major brokerage houses represent an integral element of the smart money system. Every investor should realize that there is a very close relationship between the major brokerage houses and the market makers. Some of the market maker firms are actually units of the major brokerage houses. Keep in mind that when a brokerage firm is holding a large inventory of a specific stock, it will direct its brokers to get on the phone and sell the shares with the cooperation of the NYSE specialist on the trading floor. The same would apply to the NASDAQ.

At this point, the reader should be able to use some imagination and begin to see the enormity of all this. The system has continued to evolve over the years from a single cell to a full-grown entity with a life of its own. There is a spinal structure with nerves extending throughout the entity, and there are arteries and veins leading throughout the system. The nerve system carrying information is linked throughout the body. Therefore, it becomes near impossible to declare an arm or a leg to be illegal and to be cut off. The evolution has gone on too long to allow for interference. There is fear that major surgery would lead to the bleeding to death of the system. Therefore, the establishment control system should survive as is for some time to come.

The fuel that powers the establishment control system is capital. Here is where we face some conflict between what is good for the public and what is good for the establishment structure. Our money centered establishments thrive on the inflationary forces of credit. The use of credit has granted these Wall Street institutions the power that can be used to enslave the population both physically and mentally. However morally crooked this may seem, it is all legally done with the acceptance of society. The deviant element of control over investors can easily slip right into the ensuing evolution without notice.

In his book "The Wall Street Jungle," Richard Ney stated that the principal danger to our government is not from violence or riots, but is instead from the myths which mask organized money's purposeful exploitation of the social structure. Then, he says that the interests of the Federal Reserve and the stock exchanges are not compatible with the interests of the nation's majority. This view is certainly not what is being propagated in the news media nor the textbooks of our education system.

The stock market system has become quite efficient and stable. In regards to the specialist and broker-dealer system, the typical investor is willing to overlook immorality and a total lack of ethics for the sake of a job efficiently done. While investors may believe that the efficiency in the market is specifically to serve the investor, the reality of this world dictates otherwise. Efficiency in the market is primarily a means of allowing capital inflow from investors into the brokerage centers throughout the world.

The control establishment has the resources to operate under the SEC radar system so long as the people within the system maintain their records as an invisible file. The major components of the control establishment may already have created computer software codes capable of manipulating prices and/or trading in financial markets worldwide. It is very probable that the computers at either one or more of the major investment banks may actually be able to intercept trading data. In other words, the buy and sell orders may be transmitted in micro-seconds to brokerage dealers who would allow front-running or any other types of manipulation to occur.

There is a greater and more significant picture within the picture of the market system. It comes down to the old saying of, "You cannot see the forest for the trees." While the market makers are merely agents of the brokerage establishment, it becomes possible that the brokerage components either are or can become mere agents of a greater and more powerful entity, totally invisible to public scrutiny. The art of being legally crooked has an evolution all of its own. Consider that the brokerage establishment, in the known sense of the word, is composed of corporations with stockholders and supposedly under the control of boards-of-directors.

These entities can be infiltrated with the buying of preferred stock and by other means by heavily capitalized sources. Therefore, it becomes possible that these investment banking conglomerates may become mere agents of an outside power that may not be operating under the scrutiny of the Securities and Exchange Commission. A matter for consideration may be that any such outside power, which may be linked to the brokerage establishment, may be centered anywhere in the world.

It is ironic that a control system may actually offer advantages along with the immorality of it all. It becomes a vampire-like system where it may be okay to kill and bleed many of the victims, but it is not okay to kill the majority of the victims, because the victims must survive in order to bleed them again later on in life. Therefore, good times and bad times must be orchestrated so that the control establishment can make money either way. Therefore, the objective becomes one of bleeding the investor whereby some may actually die, but the majority will live in order to maintain the species.

There may be two great factions of control that may eventually fuse together. The control establishment may be not only the investment banks but the government as well. Both of these entities strive for control over people. Therefore, it makes sense that a merging partnership may develop that will eventually totally enslave mankind. With total control over the capital system, the control establishment would justify itself for the sake of accomplishing near-perfect efficiency. It would all be legal, however immoral in its creation and operation, but it would be perceived as efficient in order to gain the cooperation of the public.

The scenario of this world order becomes easy to visualize once you observe both hands of the deceiver. In other words, the capitalist system is slowly merging with socialist ideals to form a globalization of all nations. This legally crooked system is being allowed to operate by socialist governments for the sole purpose of making those who now operate within the capitalist system to become compatible with the ideals of the socialist wealthy. The objective of both factions is the same which is total control over the public. However, the initial objective is for the socialist inclined wealthy moguls to gain control of the major investment banks throughout

21

the world. Once that is accomplished, capitalism will be able to merge with socialism to form the new world order of globalization. It all becomes a legally crooked scheme to control the world. In order to accomplish this, it may have to involve key people from both the capitalistic investment banks along with the infiltration of wealthy and influential socialist private parties. For this to come to fruition, the general population of the major nations must come under financial control.

A positive feature of financial globalization is that it tends to deter physical war between nations. A negative feature is that it dictates control over the masses of people that compose the investment network. The problem is that in order to maintain control there must be deception.

One thing is to be expected as a reaction to the study presented in this book by those reporting in the financial media. It should be simple to predict after all that has been stated here. The reader can expect all that has been stated here, and everything that has been introduced as evidence, to be rejected. The people in the financial media must protect their own financial motivations and their high paying jobs. The reader must also consider that the supporting sponsors of the financial media are the brokerage firms, the financial brokers, and the major stock exchanges. It is perfectly understandable that the sponsors of the media cannot be disparaged or alienated. The media firms are in business to make money. Therefore, the media must protect the interests of the sponsors.

4

THE MARKET MAKER SYSTEM

Why do so many professional people, who are highly successful in their own fields, fail to make money in the market? It is all very simple to understand once human motives are understood. Professional people are used to dealing with fundamental elements such as financial statements, production trends, business plans, business law, business locations, sales projections, etc. These people (doctors, lawyers, bankers, plant managers, accountants, financial consultants, etc.) are placing their faith on something tangible which is for the most part under their control. However, in the stock market, these successful business professionals may fail, because they are placing their faith in the same rules that they have been using in business. However, they fail to realize that they have no control over the price movement of stock on a stock exchange. Furthermore, they may even falsely believe that no one else does. A famous quote by John R. Keene goes as follows: "A man may know his own business and not the stock market."

In recent times, there has been more fusion in the markets due to electronic trading, and many of the terms that have been used in the past have also become fused into new definitions. While the specialist has been linked to specific NYSE stocks, the Nasdaq market makers find themselves linked to many varied stocks. In other words, a Nasdaq stock may have several market makers. However, let us be clear that a stock specialist on the NYSE is nothing more than a market maker. For the sake of this writing, we shall consider all of these people as market makers. In the past, the NYSE stock specialist has been the most powerful. However, because of the uncovering of the scams perpetrated by specialists, power is being shifted to the control establishment represented by the conglomerate investment brokerage houses. Nevertheless, it must never be forgotten that the market maker remains an arm of the establishment institutions.

While the value of your own private business can increase directly with the increased sales that you help produce, the price of the stock in the market does not necessarily follow directly with earnings or losses. The market price of a stock does not necessarily represent reality. While a public stock may be under or overvalued while being traded, a privately held business is evaluated in the realistic terms of net asset value, sales and earnings. The business owner can also physically take control of the earnings, but a public stockholder cannot do this. Many of these people who lose in the market have bought a stock that is continually earning money. If they owned the company privately, they would come out ahead. Yet, in just holding the stock, they have lost. They lost because the price of the stock has dropped despite the continued earnings of the company. These professional people have failed to realize that the price of a stock and the actual net worth of that company are not cemented together as would be the case with a privately-held concern. It is for that reason that the stock market does not represent reality. Traders are constantly either overpaying or underselling.

It is amazing that the mechanics of capitalism are so misunderstood by the majority who live under this system. To deny self-interest within oneself is as ridiculous as believing that it does not exist in those who are entrusted with political and financial power in our institutions. As a result, it can only be concluded that it is a sign of ignorance to expect any sort of stock market operator to place the interests of the public above his own except by what may be dictated by law. Being a merchant, the market maker must retail at higher prices to investors what he acquired from investors at lower prices. Unfortunately, the public does not understand this process. According to the business system, the public is traditionally expected to buy at retail. While the public buys at retail, it is the stock specialist (market maker) that sells at retail to the public.

A stock specialist, or any other form of market maker, is the "broker's broker." In other words, regular brokers bring the specialist their customers' orders to buy and sell shares of stock in which he specializes on the floor of the exchange. NYSE specialists can operate as individuals, partnerships or corporations. Most of them now operate as limited partnerships. On the other hand, the brokerage house market maker will be employed by the brokerage house. For the sake of keeping things simple, this book will consider the NYSE specialists and the brokerage house market makers to be termed as exchange operators or market makers.

The specialist system began in 1875 when James Boyd, a broker, broke his leg. Because he had to stay stationary, he limited his trading to one stock (Western Union). Before long, he had business from the public and other brokers who left orders with him for execution above or below the current price. On seeing the potential for profit, other brokers copied Boyd and specialized in specific stocks. This began a new class of people on Wall Street, perhaps the most powerful group of people in the world of stocks who derived their powers from the rules which they created in those early days. From the start, exchange operators were completely self-regulated.

The function of the specialist, according to the New York Stock Exchange, is to maintain fair and orderly markets in those stocks which he handles and to buy and sell for his own account when there is a disparity between supply and demand. As a result, he should create price continuity and liquidity in the market, and ultimately this should enable investors' orders to be executed at more favorable prices. A stock specialist is really the same as a market maker which may be employed by a brokerage house. Unfortunately, historical evidence shows that investors get executed and specialists get more favorable prices. However, this evidence does not appear on the surface and is not easily seen. As long as the specialist does his job, moral and ethical issues will not surface as far as the NYSE is concerned. The following was taken from the NYSE.

The specialists at the NYSE are employed by several firms (as of this writing). There used to be several dozen firms, but they all merged into the few that are left today. The companies listed on the major exchanges will interview employees of the specialist firms, seeking the desired people to represent them and then allow these specialists to hold inventories of the companies' stocks.

Moral codes are usually centered on the principle of conflict of interest. The specialist represents a conflict of interest primarily because he can trade for his own account. Because he can or must trade for his own account, he becomes endowed with the incentive of self-preservation and betterment. In essence, he must compete with the investor so that he can acquire stock at low prices from investors and sell stock at higher prices to other investors. It is obvious he makes money by getting stock at wholesale and selling it back at retail. Anyone with normal sense should be able to understand that basic principle.

If the market maker knows all the buy and sell orders that are above and below the current price, he can override the principle of supply and demand by applying trades for his own account. Thus, he can raise prices by buying or short-covering, or lower prices by selling or selling short. Since he knows all the stop orders, he can strive to wipe out those positions to suit his own purpose.

Up until 2002, the specialist was the only one that knew the limit buy and sell orders from his limit order book. That means that he had full control of the game for all those years. Yet, not many people even realized the implications of that situation.

The stock that is acquired at lower prices must be retailed at higher prices. This is a tedious merchandising scheme, and investors simply provide the means. Since huge amounts of stock are acquired by market makers, big blocks are usually transacted at the bottom and at the top of price movements. Therefore, big block shorting is not even made public until two weeks have gone by, and even then, the specifics of his trading are not released to the public. Considering that the public is risking capital, this kind of situation would be considered immoral and illegal in any other profession.

Unfortunately, the majority of investors do not understand the NYSE specialist system and brokerage house operators, nor do most investors even realize the system's existence. Why is there a reluctance in people to accept the reality of the method used by specialists and other operators? Perhaps to accept the idea of a rigged game would be equivalent to shattering one's dream of making it under one's own control and will.

The stock specialist runs his own business and does so with a great degree of control. The specialist is able to adapt equally as well to bull or bear markets because he is continuously buying and selling. The only difference is that he short sells much more for the long-term in a bear market while going heavier into long positions in a bull market. There will always be rallies in a bear market just as there will always be fairly large declines within a bull market.

How much do specialist firms make in a year? It was once reported in a major magazine that specialists made about 80 to 190 percent per year on their money. The NYSE was reluctant in releasing this information. When information was released, it was usually incomplete and did not show income from all operations. Furthermore, the actual earnings could be masked in many ways, with much of it being diverted to various expenses and salaries. It should easily be accepted by anyone of normal intelligence that a specialist is not going to work very long and be satisfied with a measly hundred thousand dollars per year.

A corporate or partnership specialist firm can earn millions of dollars and pay very substantial salaries to the operators. The retained earnings merely increase the power of the specialist to accumulate greater amounts of stock. These specialist firms have many millions of dollars at their disposal. After all, most of them have been in operation for many decades, and they are backed by financial institutions.

To fully comprehend the specialist operation, you must put yourself in the position of the specialist. Since you already know the basic rules and equipment, you should be able to determine what you would strive to do while in this position. In review, you would be required to make the market liquid by supplying stock to buyers and buying from sellers whenever an excess occurs. You would also maintain a book containing buy and sell orders from customers at various prices above and below the current price.

Now, if you were facing the conditions just mentioned, what would you do to make money? Would your priority be to serve the investors already in your stock, or would your priority be to maximize your ability to earn a profit? At this point, the reader should be advised that you cannot have it both ways. It is simply an idealistic fantasy to believe that these two factors can exist together when the regulations in this particular business dictate that the specialist or dealer can indeed perform operations that can create serious damage to investors.

If a specialist is legally allowed to commit an act that does cause financial damage to an investor, it would be proper for us to accept that as part of the stock market game. The situation that is not proper is that the specialist, the exchange and the media will not admit that investors can get damaged by the actions of the operators. Also, not proper is the fact that no one in the system even wants to talk about this subject. The ending result is that investors are totally in the dark and uninformed. Any writer of the sort of material found in this book would never be allowed to appear on any media station that is sponsored by exchange operators or brokerage houses. However, the stock market channels would allow psychic, zodiac and sunspot analysts to present their valuable education to the public.

What would you do to make money? Part of that question has just been answered. You would do everything possible to keep investors in the dark concerning your business. You would threaten to withdraw advertising sponsorships and you would threaten to withdraw material to fill air space. You would direct these threats to the very top managers in the business media. The media needs brokerage advertising just to exist and to increase profits.

The specialist has always accomplished at least two things at a top and at a bottom. While advancing toward a top, a specialist would sell stock from his inventory (stock bought at lower prices). This is called retailing. Once his inventory ran out, he would commence short-selling. As you can imagine, a stock can continue to rally under heavy volume. However, the specialist knew very well that heavy volume could not be sustained. He would then soak up the demand by selling short. His potential for selling short has always been quite enormous because of his available credit.

Considering that short-selling is the specialist's main tool (weapon), it is easy to see that many investors lose money while in long positions.

While so much is said regarding the protection of the public, stock specialists are allowed to sell short heavily, thereby preventing a stock from going up in price. Meanwhile, public stockholders are actually being prevented from making profits which would in the natural course be attained if the market was a true auction.

Once the advance has been halted with heavy short-selling, the specialist will want the price to drop while stockholders will want the price to go higher. The specialist will do everything in his power to lower the price by absorbing demand until a series of stop orders are hit. It is totally naïve to think that he would do otherwise.

As the decline ensues, the specialist may encounter heavy public selling. He will now use another type of strategy. By short-covering, he will now absorb the selling since short-covering involves the buying back of stock that was previously sold short. Once the specialist has covered his short positions, he will now begin buying in order to initiate the next advance.

It is easy to see from all this that rising prices create demand and that declining prices create selling. These two elements of human nature allow specialists and other smart money people to unload big blocks of stock on heavy demand at a top and allow professional operators to acquire big blocks of stock on heavy selling at a bottom.

If you owned a very big block of shares, you would be able to sell it easily in one trade if volume was heavy. On light volume, the block would have to be split into segments, or you would have to lower your asking price in order for the specialist to take it off your hands or possibly to match it up against a large institutional buy order at a lower price. The specialist has the advantage of not paying commission costs, but you would suffer a high commission cost if you tried to sell a little at a time.

The public has been brainwashed by the media and by traditional analysts into believing that increasing volume is bullish on a rally and that increasing volume is bearish on a decline. While increasing volume does push an advance along into the final stages, the public has not learned that the danger increases with the increase in volume during an advance.

It is easy to show that institutional money managers, who have been brainwashed into accepting traditional ideas, do not represent the so-called "smart money group." Who do you think is buying the big blocks from specialists and Nasdaq market makers on heavy volume at a top? That's right. The money managers of public funds are buying. Who else would be in control of such huge amounts of capital? It is the mutual funds and pension funds that do not comprehend the real world of the stock market. These fund managers may have achieved high grades in college, but unfortunately, what they learned is almost completely worthless in the market. A high school graduate, if trained properly, would do better than a college graduate in managing money. In school, people are falsely taught that stock prices are correlated with earnings, return on equity, net worth, pending fundamentals, new product programs, good news in general, etc.

The stock specialist, who stands by the trading post on the floor of the exchange, is given most of the buy and sell orders for the stock which he handles. Keep in mind that there are cooperational links with brokerage house market makers. These people are not in the dark with each other. Therefore, both factions will know where all the stops are located. This is the equivalent of telling your opponent in a game what your next move will be. What the specialist or brokerage market maker will do with all this critical information depends on the objective.

In basic terms, if a specialist wishes to accumulate, he will look at the stop orders below the current price like a hawk staring at prey. He will do everything in his power to lower the price in order to accumulate big block stop orders. His reasoning can vary. He may very well want to erase all of the stops and then initiate a short rally while distributing, followed by a sharp drop right through the same area. He will not have to acquire much inventory at those price levels where the stops were located. He will then be able to acquire the bulk of his accumulation at much lower prices.

The specialist will also observe the buy orders that are below the current price. These buy orders that are below the current price represent support. While the investor is totally in the dark, the specialist knows where the actual support is located. The specialist will often accumulate just before the level where the bulk of the buy orders is located. In so doing, he will take away the bargains from the public. Furthermore, as the stock rallies from his accumulation point, many of those people who were waiting to buy will chase the rally and help to fuel it.

On an advance, the NYSE specialist and brokerage market maker will know exactly where all the sell orders are located. In essence, he knows exactly where a rally or advance can be terminated. The sell orders from institutional funds, coupled with his own selling and short-selling, virtually guarantee that a decline will occur from a specific level.

Whenever an investor sells short, the specialist knows exactly how many shares were shorted and at what price. While the public has to be content with the short interest figures reported in the newspapers, specialists know the exact location of the short interest. So much for public disclosure!

Of course, the specialist knows very well that short-sellers will eventually buy back the stock. It will be his objective to sell that stock back to the short-sellers at higher prices. Since public short-sellers are by nature a nervous group, any rise in price will cause them to cover short positions since there is no limit for loss on the upside. Of course, the specialist is going to place importance on heavy short positions and is not going to worry about small amounts of short interest. The stock specialist is the only true master of the short sale, and he should not be challenged since he is holding most of the aces with jokers in reserve.

Things do change with time, and it is true that traders now have access to the buy and sell orders in real time. OpenBook was introduced in January of 2002, and it does allow traders off the NYSE floor to see the buy and sell orders at each price level for all securities. Investors can observe the listing at home from their own Internet brokerage website. Prior to that regulation, investors could only see the present bid and offer. At this point, it seems as if the specialists and other market makers have lost their key weapon. However, if you observe the display of the orders in the book, it may strike you that the ability to be well trained may still rest with the professional eye of the market maker. To the average investor, the speed of the movement of the buy and sell figures in the book may come to feel like a mind-boggling mess. As a result, the specialist or market maker simply has to adjust the operation slightly to protect the ability to maintain the advantage.

The following entry is a blog statement that I placed on the internet to explain the changes in the power structure between the NYSE specialists and the brokerage house specialists. Brokerage house trading operators are really specialists. They are usually termed as market makers. In reality, the brokerage house market maker has become the same as the formerly defined stock specialist. They all do the same thing. They are there to make money for their own systems. Yes, there was a change in power from 2004 to 2008. Power shifted to the major brokerage houses. However, with the financial collapse in late 2008 into early 2009, the major brokerage houses came under disruption. There were mergers, buyouts, etc. This caused something to happen which the average person did not see. While it seemed like the major brokerage houses were worthless, there were a few entities that had the capital to buy out the firms in trouble with the blessing of the U.S. Government. Goldman-Sachs and J.P. Morgan did rather well. A few of the major banks also got the chance to acquire some of the major brokerage house facilities. For example, Bank of America got Merrill Lynch.

Tuesday, December 16, 2008
Stock Market Reality: Legally Crooked
by Anthony Campos

For years I have been preaching about the crookedness of the stock market. I said that the stock specialist system was crooked, and I was proven correct in the years 2004 through 2008. When the specialist firms began to crumble under each government probe, I stated that the problem was not going to be solved. I stated on my website that one crooked system was going to be replaced with another crooked system. As one crooked entity goes out, another will take its place. The evolution of this process actually creates a more sophisticated system of moral corruption. While investors are made to believe that the expulsion of a crooked entity is a great accomplishment, they do not see reality through the illusion. As one crook is sacrificed by the system, a more evolved form of the virus takes over.

Unfortunately, the crooks of Wall Street operate with a license, an SEC license. This is what makes the whole system legally crooked. The issuance of an SEC license makes it legal while the lack of ethics and morality makes it crooked. The greed to make money by whatever means seems to supersede the satisfaction of being moral and ethical.

Consider that analysts are employed by brokerage houses and that many of these are now owned by banks and other major financial institutions. Do you truly believe that there is no problem with this system of doing business?

Consider also that the futures market which trades when the NYSE is closed during the night is traded on such light volume that people with capital power can easily control the price. Do you think that maybe there is not a problem with this? There are times when the overnight futures are either way up or way down. The media will always have an excuse for this. However, consider also that the stock market channels are also under the control of powerful financial institutions such as GE.

When all of these things are considered, you should easily realize that it does not require a master detective to detect a strong possibility of foul play. The market is geared to deceive investors into doing the wrong thing. While at the top of a bull market, both analysts and the media get people to invest fully. While at the bottom of a bear market, it becomes the reverse. I find it amazing that both the analysts and the media may be employed by those who are doing the exact opposite of what the investors are being told to do.

33

Concluding Remarks

If the specialist system should disappear, some other form of deviant power will take its place. The investing public should not revel at the thought of an electronic or digital system, because such a system will have more capacity to completely hide deviant acts. Keep in mind that humans can be held directly responsible and pinpointed with guilt, whereas an electronic system may not be so easy to figure out. Furthermore, at this point in time, it is not fully known the extent of power that may rest with the Nasdaq market makers and their affiliated firms. However, all market makers should come under suspicion after all that has been experienced on the NYSE. The power of collusion within the control establishment may be extensive because there is a lack of vigilance in this regard. It is for that reason that the control establishment has the ability and the resources to manipulate the markets in a much more refined manner than the specialists could ever imagine. The fall of the specialist empire becomes a blessing for the big investment banking firms. In this evolutionary process, the power has manifested itself within a more powerful conglomerate of talented people with widespread connections throughout the government, and the power of capital resources has been retained under direct control. There is an old saying that one crook will always be willing to kill another crook to retain more power.

The reader should keep in mind that the control establishment will emphasize that there are hundreds of regulations in this industry. However, the investment bank establishment will never tell you that vigilance and enforcement can be circumvented by hundreds of loopholes and circumstances. It will never admit that there exists a gray area of deception.

5

OPENBOOK CONNECTION

Whenever a control establishment entity does something which is supposed to help the investor, it should be expected that it is instead meant to help itself. Imagine what it would be like at a general meeting of the NYSE elites. Would one of the members simply say that it is time to help investors make more money by allowing them to understand better how we have been taking advantage them, and therefore, we should now level the playing field so that they will be able to share in some of the profit that we have been making all this time. At this point, the members of the NYSE central committee would most likely be sitting there staring at you. Is that how it would go?

Now, let us consider the following instead. "There is indication that the SEC is going to begin investigations into our specialist system, and maybe it is time for us to begin to make it look good, and so maybe we should give the investor a tidbit, and in the process, we can make some extra money." At this point, the members would perk up at the idea of making some extra money by giving a tidbit. How does that sound?

In January 2001, the NYSE completed the switch from fractions to the decimal system. Because there were now more increments of price levels, there was more demand for the transparency of depth from the bid and ask price. As a result, the NYSE began work on a plan to release the limit orders from the specialists' books and other electronic sources publicly. OpenBook was introduced in January 2002. This means that the specialist can no longer keep the buy and sell orders secret. However, the investor should keep in mind that a market maker is not obligated to place his buy and sell orders on the book.

The OpenBook event was touted with great fanfare, and it was promoted as a great event for the investor. The NYSE Magazine even presented a quote by Myles Gillespie, president of Fleet Meehan Specialist, as saying, "Any effort to build transparency can only strengthen our market." At this point, the reader should consider the workings of human motivation. Why would a specialist be in favor of giving up a market advantage? Well, the motivation may involve one or two good reasons, and perhaps even more hidden reasons may be involved.

First of all, the specialist firms were already coming under investigation by the Justice Department for improper trading. Something had to be done to show that the NYSE was not performing illegal acts behind closed doors. A move to open the specialist's book would come across as a sign that there was no intent of wrongdoing. Such a move represents pure common sense by the NYSE accompanied by the blessing of all the specialists.

Secondly, but perhaps of primary importance, it always seems to come down to money. The NYSE charges a fee for OpenBook (Boehmer, Saar, & Yu, 2004). Commercial vendors and large broker-dealers take the data from the NYSE and pay $5,000 per month, and then, the NYSE also receives $50 per month from each subscriber who gets the service from the vendor. By the end of 2003, the NYSE was making about $870,000 per month from this service, and the revenue continues to increase. This is what you call helping mankind.

The researchers, Boehmer, Saar and Yu (2004), go on to report the following, all of which is important. The cancellation of limit orders increases after OpenBook is initiated, and traders begin to use smaller orders instead of large blocks. In other words, public traders have more fear of exposing their own intentions. This whole affair becomes ironic. Before the initiation of OpenBook, investors feared the specialist, and now, traders fear each other.

Harris (1996) theorizes even prior to OpenBook that there are two risks associated with the exposure of limit orders. The first is that a trader may reveal information about the value of a security, and the second is that traders may break up their orders into smaller blocks, and perhaps make use of floor brokers to manage the trades instead of adding their orders to the limit orders on the book.

Now, let us consider other problems. If the market suddenly declines, traders may not enter the market if they see small orders under the market which would signal that the market could go into a big sell-off. Since the specialist would easily observe all of this, he could now short into the buy orders knowing full well that investors were holding back.

It is important to understand that OpenBook does not include the specialist's proprietary trading interest nor that of the floor broker (Boehmer et al., 2004). This means that OpenBook does not indicate total depth in the market. Furthermore, OpenBook does not provide any order execution capabilities. The illusion of grandeur does not end there.

Where are all the smart people? They must all be working for the control establishment. Stop orders to sell or buy do not show up on a limit order book. However, specialists or other market makers know where they are located. Is this a critical factor? When a stop order is hit, the order becomes a market order, and it is executed immediately at whatever price is available. Stop-limit orders do show up on OpenBook, and these can only be executed at the price that is listed. Sell short orders will show up if they are filed as limit orders. At this point, investors should simply realize that stop orders are not the same as stop-limit orders.

Before the celebration continues in this effort to serve mankind (perhaps on a dish), it turns out that learning how to use the limit orders in OpenBook probably takes some time, and this is true for both traders that wish to optimize the execution of orders and for traders who want to design profitable trading strategies (Boehmer et al., 2004). Whatever the case, a little experience in the observation of price movement on OpenBook will quickly discourage the average trader. The first time a very large sell order disappears before your eyes followed by the price going higher, you will lose your enthusiasm for OpenBook. While it may be interesting to see all the limit orders, the fact remains that it may tend to cause more damage to traders since the market maker is much better trained to use the book. Who is really in control of the limit order book? He who controls the field will always be the winner.

Traders should also realize that there are two trading mechanisms for large block trades. A block can be sent directly to the "downstairs" market where it would show up on the limit order list. However, in some cases, a large block of stock may be directed to the "upstairs" market, where a block dealer will locate a seller or buyer and then cross the trade according to regulations on the tape. A block broker may easily be able to negotiate a better price (Madhavan, 2002).

While some traders may revel at the idea of using OpenBook based on transparency, the fact remains that many studies show that too much pre-trade transparency could reduce liquidity and cause traders not to reveal their intentions (Madhavan, Porter, & Weaver, 2000). What may be good for one trader may not be good for another. Either way, the establishment comes out a winner by making the show that it is accommodating all traders.

When all of the evidence is considered, the specialist has not really given up all that much. Furthermore, it may not have been disclosed to the public if whether or not specialists were granted special concessions for agreeing to OpenBook. Keep in mind that the NYSE is making revenue from the OpenBook service. With all the facts considered, it may even be that specialists and all other market makers are better off with every new system that is initiated by the NYSE in the name of serving mankind. All of these programs that are initiated are legally crooked because they are touted as being for the good of the investor while actually being better for those who engineer the product.

6

RESEARCH STUDIES

Many studies have been done by researchers concerning stock specialists, Nasdaq market makers, and brokerage analysts. These studies have been done by doctorate type people who have done rather elaborate quantitative operations using valid statistical methodology. While many of these studies may not reveal anything of an illegal nature, these studies do reveal that the basics mentioned in this book, concerning the market maker, are indeed true. These studies which represent peer-reviewed work, backed by actual research in the field, clearly prove that stock specialists along with other types of market makers possess a decisive advantage over the public trader. These works are presented here in order to reinforce the reader that the principles of the state of being legally crooked are not just a fantasy of conspiracy theories.

Secondly, the work of this book is not complete without mentioning the work of Richard Ney who passed away on July 18, 2004. This man was a pioneer in revealing, with many examples of evidence, that showed the extent of a crooked specialist system. He wrote three books concerning the specialist system, and he was an investment advisor. Just before his death, he got his satisfaction in the news that the specialist firms were being taken into court for improprieties. However, in the years before that event, the media continued to defend the specialists and would not allow Richard Ney to openly go on the air. The commentators on CNBC treated the subject as a conspiracy theory. Because of that attitude, the media will find no mercy with this writer. My testimony is that I witnessed the reaction from commentators after one of Ney's TV presentations. The media was at the time just as legally crooked as the system that it defended.

At this time, it is totally in order to mention the attributes of human nature. In very simple form, it is human nature to abuse power. If the reader cannot understand that very simple rule of nature, then it is better for the reader, at this point, to retire back into the world of fantasy and naivety. This is the real world out here.

The following quote comes from the research done by Sigridur Benediktsdottir, who was at the time an economist in the Division of International Finance of the Board of Governors of the Federal Reserve System. The public has a right to know his exact words. Benediktsdottir (2006) did the research using valid statistical measurements, and he concluded his journal paper as follows:

> It is quite noteworthy to see that when specialists are not performing their trading obligations by being on the opposite side of a market, they are in almost eighty-five percent of the trades buying low and selling high. This is the most convincing evidence supporting the theory that specialists are informed about future price movements.

Research also verifies that any losses by specialists tend to be involved with operations while trying to keep the market liquid, but specialists tend to make a profit while doing self-initiated trades (Benediktsdottir, 2006). This result does justify their existence. In other words, it is okay to take a loss on liquidity trading, because it will look good in the eyes of the New York Stock Exchange. In order to make up for any such losses, the specialist has to make money on his own market trades, and those profits must go beyond any of the losses. This does make sense. The public should realize that the market maker is not a public servant.

Academic research into the operations of a stock specialist goes back a long time. Bowlin and Rozeff (1987), using the quantitative methodology, stated in their research report that there is evidence of market inefficiency because the specialists' short sale ratio has been able to predict stock returns for well over forty years prior to this date. They say that the results are not random and that average stock returns are significantly higher after low values of the ratio than they are after high values of the ratio. This should be proof enough that shorting by specialists has been backed up by some force, whether it be by their own manipulation or by some other force. Either way, the specialist was well informed concerning the future. Bowlin and Rozeff (1987) do conclude by saying that the specialists' short sale ratio may not be valid into the future, perhaps because of regulation changes, only that it has had power in the past.

You may already know that the short sale has always been the main tool of the specialist, because it carries hardly any restriction. If a trader wishes to buy a huge block of stock, and not enough stock is available at the time, it stands to reason that the specialist should have the ability to accommodate that trader by shorting the stock on paper alone. After such trade, the specialist has time to actually find the stock.

Madhavan and Smidt (1992), using quantitative measures of specialist trades and quotes, stated that order imbalances convey signals to the specialist regarding future price movements where the specialist appears to possess market information unavailable to most traders. In the method used for this research, they say that future order imbalances affect current price quotations. They go on to say that large block trades appear to convey little information to the specialist, because those blocks may have been anticipated by the specialist through 'leakage' in the upstairs market. Once again, we see a research report that leans in that same direction which is that stock specialists do have powers well above any of those possessed by the average trader. Again, the conclusion can only be that it is legally crooked.

Angel (1997) tended to confirm in a highly detailed research report that short selling by the public does not represent people that are better informed than any other traders. This deserves some mention here because this represents public short selling which is in reverse to specialist short selling. In other words, public shorting is bullish for the market while specialist short selling tends to indicate bearishness for the market. The reader of this should immediately see that the stock market works upside down to human comprehension, which is why it becomes an illusion that is used by the control establishment to entice the average investor to do the wrong thing. In conclusion, Angel (1997) stated that short sale orders have the same or significantly less effect on subsequent quotes and trades than do regular sale orders. The market maker is the only true master of the short sale, except for those individuals that possess the power to use huge amounts of capital and are well informed about the future.

It is a common belief that there are many market makers for any Nasdaq stock and that when an order is placed, the buy or sell order goes out to every available dealer in order to get the best execution for the investor. In reality, Paul Schultz (2003) stated that there might be far fewer market makers who are able to make a market in a stock because of competitive advantages as deemed by your own brokerage firm. He is saying that your order for a Nasdaq stock is seldom sent to a market maker on the basis of a quoted price. The implication here is quite simple. While you may get a better price from a particular dealer, your order will be sent to a dealer that holds favoritism with your brokerage firm. Of course, this sort of procedure can only be considered legally crooked.

Furthermore, Schultz goes on to say that a market maker that provides analyst coverage is more likely to have non-public information or more likely to anticipate news releases than a market maker who does not provide coverage. He also states that the market maker is also more likely to obtain information about a stock through conversations with the firm's employees if the company is localized. He also confirms that a market maker may be well informed if the company has gone through a stock offering with the brokerage firm.

Researchers Kee Chung and Seong-Yeon Cho (2005) stated outright in their report that analysts recommend stocks to help their brokerage dealer, rather than to help investors, and that it is important that investors use caution when advisories are given. They further agree that analysts have an incentive to promote those stocks that are handled by affiliated market makers by providing information concerning the release of buy or sell recommendations. While the Justice Department may take the time to investigate an investor who may have bought or shorted a huge amount of stock just prior to a news release, the cronies of the government will never bother to investigate if whether or not the market maker has acquired an unusual amount of stock either long or short.

Although not directly related to anything that may be legally crooked, but perhaps only indirectly related, is the shorting activity of the Nasdaq compared to the NYSE. Benjamin Blau, Bonnie Van Ness, and Robert Van Ness (2011) researched together to determine how shorting on the Nasdaq compared to that of the NYSE. They confirmed that shorting on the Nasdaq is significantly greater than short selling on the NYSE. They further confirmed the conclusion of Theissen (2000) that short sellers on the Nasdaq are better able to predict negative returns than short sellers on the NYSE. This conclusion falls in line with the conclusion of Blau et al. that short sellers on the Nasdaq are better at predicting negative next-day returns than the NYSE short sellers. This means that Nasdaq stocks tend to become more out of line with their true fundamental value than NYSE stocks which attract more contrarian informed short selling. The analysis of this situation is now up to the reader to determine. We can say that Nasdaq stocks are simply more volatile. We can say that the dealer system of the Nasdaq is simply not as efficient as that of the NYSE auction system.

Let us be clear about the value of all these research reports. The findings of these researchers are valid, and their conclusions are correct. However, there may be other conclusions that can be added to those of the researcher without countering the findings. In the case of the Nasdaq short sellers, we could very well add that short selling is very profitable on the Nasdaq which opens up the idea that crookedness may be involved. In other words, targeted Nasdaq stocks are being heavily shorted by certain parties that may be associated with brokerage powers such as upper management executives and analysts of various financial firms. Then, with the help of negative news on a particular day, the short sellers can easily make fifty percent or more on a sharp decline in the stock. If this was to occur on the NYSE, it would attract attention. Therefore, the findings of this research can be indirectly tied to legally crooked activity. It is legal because nothing can be proven, and it is crooked because many investors are left holding long positions on huge downward gaps in the price of the stock.

All of this tends to indicate that someone is making huge amounts of money by shorting Nasdaq stocks just as the specialists of the NYSE made huge amounts of money on shorting their own stocks. In the case of the Nasdaq, the difference is quite pronounced. In other words, the amount of capital involved on these Nasdaq short selling transactions clearly outpaces the shorting by NYSE specialists. It should make one wonder, where the financing comes from to back up the short selling, and one may also question why are these people so well informed.

7

BROKERAGE ANALYSTS

A brokerage analyst works for and is paid by a brokerage firm. This person is certainly not an independent party. It is amazing that the investing public so easily accepts this system without question. In any other form of business, such an arrangement would surely be questioned. Consider the ramifications of this arrangement. The brokerage establishment hires both the analyst and the market maker. It becomes a simple logic that all three facets of this operation will know what each other is doing or intends to do at all times.

Much research has been done by private parties regarding brokerage analysts. There are also many opinions that have been expressed both by academic researchers and by people from within the brokerage industry. The bulk of the research and professional opinions seem to point in one direction, which is that there is both bias and collusion within the brokerage establishment. To be fair, statements that are presented here will be referenced with credible sources whenever possible. This work shall proceed from evidence to logical conclusions.

In July 2002, the NYSE (Rule 472) and NASD (Rule 2711) adopted regulation designed to cut the ties between the investment banking and research departments within investment banks, or in other words, brokerage firms that can offer the securities of companies going public. These regulations were meant to stop any bias that may occur for analysts to give a pass for securities being offered by the investment banking firm that hired them. Overall, this meant that brokerage analysts could not communicate with people from the banking department, and it also meant that the salary of the analyst could not be related to any stock offering.

These regulations came about because of all the complaints that were pouring in by investors. Furthermore, researchers in the field, namely Ph.D. scholars were clearly showing that affiliated analysts, who are from investment banks with an existing relationship with either the brokerage firm or firm that is selling the securities, tend to show more optimistic bias than unaffiliated analysts (Michaely & Womack, 1999). However, this collusion had been known for decades, and it was considered legal. The only revelation here is that the government officially recognized this particular problem, but in recognizing this problem, the government failed to recognize the main problem which is the collusion between the analyst and the market maker.

On April 23, 2003, the Global Research Settlement was reached between the New York Attorney General's Office, the SEC, the NYSE, the NASD, and twelve investment related banking firms. This settlement required a huge fine. Furthermore, it banned analysts from going on road trips with investment bankers, and it increased the IPO "quiet period" from 25 to 40 days. However, in trying to solve one problem, there will almost always be consequences. In this case, it becomes probable that a migration of talented analysts will occur out of the major brokerage firms which may actually provide less quality in the information presented to investors (Clarke, Khorana, Patel, & Rau, 2009).

The new regulations concerning investment banker analysts and the Global Research Settlement amount to a magic show of illusions. It is possible that the major brokerage firms are actually very satisfied that the regulations only involved investment banking and not the trading business. In other words, the spotlighted show diverted attention away from the control system machine. In one sense, the new laws make the investment banker look good in the eyes of the investor. The investment banker can now state that all analysis is completely independent. Meanwhile, the brokerage house is making huge amounts of money off the relationship between the analyst and the brokerage market maker. The conclusion of this should be obvious. A good magician will divert your attention toward a direction that is opposite where your eyes should be. While you are busy paying attention to what amounts to nonsense, the magician will protect his secret.

Whether or not the new laws really accomplished the goal of making analysts independent remains to be proven. Investors must realize that the people who work in the field of the securities market are highly talented in their ability to adapt. This ability is so creative that it can work its way around just about any law that may be passed. In very simple terms, it is the ability to be legally crooked.

The law says that there can be no communication between the analyst and the investment banking department. On a particular day, a certain analyst is chosen that is keen to the system and is given a request to research a particular company that is going public. It becomes clear to that particular analyst where this request originated. Beyond this point, there is no need to confer with the investment banking department. If the job is done right, this particular analyst will get an added bonus for doing something else that is not covered by the new law.

There is one big positive feature concerning the Global Research Settlement. It did officially prove that brokerage analysts have always been guilty of collusion in showing bias in their presentations to get investors to buy into stock offerings. If the people within a brokerage firm have always been able to conspire when a stock offering comes about, then where does the conspiracy end? Any form of logic that may be applied here should dictate that there must be many more important and critical links between the management of the various brokerage houses. Furthermore, it becomes obvious that this form of communication tips the balance of power away from the investor. The end result is that money which is lost by the public will find its way to those that have the control of inside information and can legally act upon that information. The Securities and Exchange Commission sponsors the power that makes it all legally crooked.

Analyst Stock Coverage

The real issue to be addressed involves not investment banking, but the advice from the analyst for stocks in general. Are analysts really any good at what they do? To answer this question, one must really consider each phase of what occurs in the price from just before the event, right after

47

the event, and out to several months after the event of the advice. Much research has been done on this topic. For example, Michaely and Womack (2007) stated that analysts' recommendations based on long-term high growth optimism inevitably disappoint and that they are directionally correct in the post-event period only about 54% of the time.

When a brokerage analyst does an upgrade, the price may go up immediately which is understandable. Then, the price may drift upward for a few months (Michaely & Womack, 2007). This means that the greatest kick occurs when the analyst releases the upgrade, and the greatest decline occurs when a downgrade is released. It becomes obvious that the investors who buy on that advice will be paying a higher price. To make real money, an investor has to buy or short before the analyst releases the advice. If stock is being held that has advanced on an upgrade, it becomes advisable to consider selling over a period of a few days to allow for profit taking.

This is what occurs. The market maker knows of the upgrade or downgrade. If it is an upgrade, the market maker will buy inventory in anticipation of increased buying volume. This is all legal because it is his job to comply with supply and demand requirements. Certainly, if the price goes up on increased volume demand, the job of the specialist or Nasdaq market maker is to be prepared to supply stock into that demand in order to maintain an orderly market. Once the market maker unloads his inventory, which may take a few days, he will short and take prices lower. Then, after a while, he will cover shorts and accumulate, and he will take the price higher in order to make the brokerage advice look good for a few months. Eventually, when the price forms a top, the analyst will still be sitting there at the highest level of buying advice while the market maker goes short. The downgrade will then occur once the price has declined substantially. This is how brokerage firms make real money.

One research report by Torngren and Montgomery (2004) concluded outright that results from testing show that the information-based predictions of the professionals do not outperform the simple logic used by laypeople. However, keep in mind the general theory behind the illusion in the marketplace. Because investors tend to forget past events amidst the array of news items being released, the brokerage analysts are out to make money for the company and to be rewarded for meeting an objective. Since investors' memories may be short, analysts can get away with revising their initial flawed projections and use other means to prop up a stock (Agrawal & Chen, 2005).

The statements within this paragraph are referenced by Jegadeesh and Kim (2004) and are totally in accord with the philosophy of this book. Sell and strong sell recommendations in all nations are less than that of buy and strong buy recommendations, and the frequency of sell advice by analysts is lowest in the U.S. It may be that the new regulations coming from the restrictions placed on analysts may lead to more sell recommendations. However, investors should not ponder on this, because strong sell recommendations can be very damaging to the stockholders of that particular stock. A brokerage firm that issues a sell recommendation may make enough money on selling short to make up for any loss of friendship with a corporation. Keep in mind that the board-of-directors may already know of any downgrades that may be forthcoming. Finally, analysts will most likely not perform any better despite the effort to remove any conflicts of interest. The reason for this is simple. The performance of brokerage analysts is based primarily on their ability to make money for the brokerage house while the investor remains in second place.

The analyst is not out to receive glory in the news. His only glory comes from within the company by doing his share to increase the trading volume by brokerage clients. It becomes easy to see that not many can do this job. For the sake of receiving a big bonus, these people will easily discredit humility, ethics, and whatever else has to be done. After all, no laws are actually broken. This is all simply a case of being legally crooked.

Generating Trading Volume

Researchers have also done much work involving the true objective of the analyst. Although a large brokerage house makes money in many various ways, trading volume by its clients becomes crucial. Profits cannot be produced if clients merely hold for long term purposes. When a large brokerage firm has many trading clients, its analysts will be called upon to work harder to initiate stock upgrades. One way to increase trading volume is for the analyst to issue an optimistic forecast, and another way is for the analyst to revise a prior forecast, or possibly reiterate a prior forecast (Agrawal & Chen, 2005).

Research journals can easily be found that corroborate the statements that are made here. This research comes from many Ph.D. writings concerning the importance of the analyst. From work done on the Toronto Stock Exchange, Irvine (2001) determined that brokers trade more shares and have higher market shares in covered stocks than they do in uncovered stocks and that on average, brokers increase their market shares in covered stock by 3.8% as compared to uncovered stocks. He goes on to conclude that Canadian brokerage firms do compensate analysts on the amount of commission revenue that is generated in the stocks that are covered.

At first glance of this whole situation concerning the generation of trading, one might believe that it is okay since stockholders that were holding going into the upgrade are better off. However, those who are buying on the upgrade may not do as well since they are paying more for the stock. The problem with all of this is that no one is considering how much the brokerage firm is making because no one on the outside knows what positions were acquired by the brokerage prior to the upgrade. Furthermore, it is possible that the brokerage may have links to hedge funds that may not be legally connected to the brokerage firm that is doing the upgrade.

In the case of a downgrade, the situation becomes detrimental to the stockholders of the stock. It also becomes detrimental to stockholders that may be clients of the brokerage firm doing the downgrade, which is the equivalent of throwing clients to the lions. Meanwhile, the brokerage firm is making money on the short position taken by the market makers, and perhaps, the firm is also making money by its outside connections.

All of these methods of deception and deviant behavior have been worked out by company attorneys who are masters of the gray area of the law. These are all examples of events that are not noticed nor observed by the public. Furthermore, the mainstream media would even go so far as to call any criticism as being a conspiracy theory. As you can see, the control establishment seems to have it all on their side. This is how the system can survive without much complaint. Every angle that is employed by the control establishment seems to fall under the classification of being legal. While this writer places emphasis on what may be considered unethically crooked, the media places emphasis on what may be considered legal.

8

STOCK OPTIONS AND FUTURES

The options and futures on the Dow Industrials Average index have been trading on the Chicago Board of Trade since October 6, 1997, with the S&P going much further back. Both the Dow and S&P are the most widely followed averages, and are, therefore, the most important targets for the control establishment.

Stock index futures and the process of options expiration, along with rumor mills, are the biggest tools used by the Wall Street control establishment. It is amazing that so many tools are available to the brokerage industry that can be employed to deceive and manipulate the public. A stock specialist is allowed to trade in the stock options of the issues which he maintains. The reasoning for this is that specialists should be allowed to hedge positions. However, the real issue is something else altogether. Those who wish to study illusionology, as it relates to the stock market, should always consider the relativity between entities within the market. There is relativity between the analyst, the market maker, the brokerage management, and all of the other departments of the firm including options and futures trading. Within the brokerage network, the use of stock options and futures represents powerful tools that can be used by the control establishment.

Those who control the market need only control the stocks that lead in each sector. Going a step further, it can then be said that those who control the market need only make use of certain vehicles that can exert influence on the market. By using these methods, it would not take very much capital to make the market move. Once a spark is ignited, the public will jump to it. One can only admire how well this whole system is calibrated. The whole market system becomes much like an orchestra under the leadership of a conductor.

Stock and Index Options

First of all, the market maker can realistically only use options in a limited way when hedging. He may use options as a hedge for small amounts of stock. This will usually occur when he supplies stock by shorting or absorbs stock by buying, and he knows very well that the trend will continue longer. However, these are for fairly small trades. We know very well that the smart money people deal in large blocks near tops and bottoms. It would take too many options just to hedge a few big block positions since one option equals one hundred shares.

It makes more sense for the brokerage market maker to communicate with management, who will then communicate with the analyst, that a certain stock will not go above a certain price or vice versa. Upon knowing this information, the brokerage management can then notify the options department to write calls or puts that will most likely never be exercised. People that buy out-of-the-money options will simply take their chances. It makes sense for the market maker to create options on a short-term basis by writing them against long term holdings when his stock is simply in a holding pattern. It also makes sense for the specialist firm or market maker to acquire options at certain expiration dates for the purpose of acquiring stock at those expiration dates.

There are certain issues that do display a rather curious peculiarity at the expiration. In these issues, the price of the stock tends to gyrate to a particular strike price on the options on the day of expiration. For example, the price will quite often close on expiration at either 155, 160 or 165 which would correspond to a strike price. Be on the lookout for this.

One time I had several CPQ call options with a strike price of 30. The stock rallied a little into the last week but would not go above 30. When expiration day arrived, it just sat there at 30 as the options expired worthless. It was frustrating to watch. However, guess what happened in the following session after expiration? CPQ advanced by a significant amount. This was not just a coincidence. I have over the years seen this type of phenomena occur over and over again in certain key issues. In another instance, I had Intel call options with a strike of 70. Intel closed on expiration at 70. On the following session, it made an advance of several points. Therefore, it is quite obvious that there is a force acting on the stock's price at expiration. Option traders should watch out for this force which could seriously affect their position. Needless to say, I lost everything on those options. As a result, I firmly believe that options on a particular stock should expire every three months. There is no doubt in my mind that the monthly expiration of stock options is very detrimental to investors. There may be many investors that simply do not take note of stock options, and as a result, they may make a bad decision based only on the stock price.

In conclusion, the specialist will not use options to hedge when at a top or bottom, because he already knows it to be a reversal point. At reversal points, specialists are selling their put options to the public at the bottom, or they are selling call options to the public at the top. This system works very well for the specialist because the public does the opposite. However, by using hedging as a reason, it does accomplish one thing. It gives the impression that specialists take horrible risks for the good of investors. The fact remains that market makers may know that there may be a huge amount of overhead stock ready to sell that does not show up on the book.

We have been talking about specialists, but a brokerage house market maker has now become even more powerful since the brokerage market maker is operating under somewhat different rules. A brokerage house is a big concern with many different departments. This means that a brokerage house can acquire call and put options and can write options (create them) without coming under the same scrutiny as a specialist. Keep in mind that while there is only one specialist for a particular stock, there may be many market makers for any one particular stock. We are talking about market makers that are under the roof of the big brokerage houses that have plenty of money. Many of the big brokerage houses are also owned by some of the biggest banks. You should be able to see the power that these people can generate as compared to the old specialist system.

54

Options expiration will occur on almost every Friday of every month. Here is where certain irregularities may occur. As the expiration date gets closer, option holders that have stock tied to the deal will unwind their positions. If you can use some imagination here, you should be able to see that stock will either be bought or sold in order to unwind positions involving options which are due to expire. There will be times when the stock price will gyrate to the call options with the greatest open interest. There will be times when the stock price will just sit there and go nowhere for several days. This type of event can be very detrimental to the stockholders who sell their stock at options expiration not knowing about how this system works. This is just another example of an event that is highly legally crooked.

One more thing should be said concerning options trading. It is addictive and should be avoided unless one can truly control greed and anxiety. Although it is possible to acquire fortunes in a very short period of time with options, this writer is giving fair warning that such a trend in making money cannot be sustained. No matter how good you may be in the analysis of accumulation and distribution, you can never employ in a consistent manner the timing that is required in order to buy something such as an option which has an expiration time limit. The odds are simply not good over the long term. The problem is that not many people are able to buy either calls or puts only in those cases that are truly rare situations where the odds may be slightly in favor. Options should only be used when the indicators in market maker analysis are very strong to either the upside or downside. The greed to make fast money in options is simply highly addictive.

Conservative Strategies

Investors that have a more substantial amount of capital in the market should consider a different approach. Instead of merely buying calls and puts, one should consider writing options against a stock position. After all, the people that really make money are those who create options. Why is this? Well, they say that 80% to 90% of all options expire worthless. These options that expire worthless are created by people who profit in having the options expire worthless. For example, if you have one hundred shares of a

55

stock, you can write and sell a call option against your hundred shares and receive a premium. That premium now becomes yours to keep. If that option expires worthless, you get to keep the stock, and the premium becomes your profit. It is true that you could lose a certain amount by having to give up your stock at the call option strike price, but the odds are in your favor over the long term. If done properly, this strategy can be considered excellent.

Another strategy might be to protect your stock position. This would act much like an insurance policy. For example, if your stock was at $71.50, you could buy a put option with a strike of 70 for say $1.80. That situation would limit your downside risk while keeping your upside unlimited. In this case, your maximum loss would be $3.30 per share. You would lose the $1.80 that you paid for the put, and you would lose $1.50 off your stock price for having it exercised at 70. That is good insurance if you are mildly bullish, but may be worrisome about any near-term decline.

Have you ever wondered where all those options come from? Thousands and thousands of options are always hitting the market. Most of them are being created by the exchange insiders who have huge amounts of stock and make extra money while holding that stock by writing options for a premium. They already have assurances that the options which are written on their stock will expire worthless. This means that they make a profit equal to the price of the options which were sold to the public. That is why so many people lose on options, and that is why so many options expire worthless.

A Special Situation

Consider the following situation. This is a conservative play using call options which many investors do not realize. You are interested in an intermediate-term play on a stock going for $62. It is January. You search for all the monthly call options with a strike of 60. The nearby call options may run 2.50 to 3.00 while a twelve-month option could run $4. If you bought one hundred shares, it would cost you $6,200. You would make $100 per point on the upside, and your downside would be unlimited right down to zero.

You could buy the call option for next January with a strike of 60 for $400. Now, look at this closely. Your downside is limited to the price of the option. In other words, you could lose all $400. However, even if the stock went down more than four points, your option would still have some sort of premium, because it would only expire on the following January.

If the stock goes above 64, your option would have a real value of at least $400 at expiration so long as it stays above 64. Every point on the upside would now produce $100 which is the same as if you had bought the stock. Buying the stock would cost you $6,200, and buying the call option would cost you $400. The commission cost would be nominal either way.

As you can see, even if the stock dropped down to 58 in a few weeks, your option would still be worth a premium, but if you had the stock, you would be four points down or minus $400.

As a final note, you should know that stock options are not reported to the IRS by your broker. Your broker will send you a report of all your trades. It will be up to you to report your option trades on your tax forms. You should learn as much as possible about options. Option trading should be done responsibly. Learn to keep the odds in your favor. Do not just believe the misconception that options should not be considered because they are dangerous. Call and put options can be used conservatively to improve your odds if you are willing to learn how to use them properly. Finally, because options expiration tends to cause stock prices to level off at certain strike price levels, investors who do not know about options can be damaged by either selling or buying the stock based on the leveling of the price, while stock exchange operators, being more knowledgeable, can take advantage of investors. This, in itself, can be considered legally crooked.

Stock Index Futures: The Ultimate Legally Crooked Tool

Stock index futures are open all day long. This particular issue becomes of primary importance because the futures control the market in the short term. This means that if an entity has the power to move the futures, then the movement of the market can be controlled in the short term.

57

It is amazing that no one in the financial media will touch this issue. Even a raggedly, streetwise kid from the back alleys of Bogotá, Columbia would sense that something was wrong here. This issue involving the Dow and S&P futures is so far legally crooked that anyone of normal intelligence should realize that the playing field is far from being level. Trading the futures, when the stock market cannot trade, should be banned.

Robbani and Bhuyan (2005) show from an elaborate study that the volatility of the market significantly increased after the start of futures and options trading on the Dow Jones Industrial Average index. It is found that a significant increase in volatility occurs in the majority of the Dow stocks. However, it is concluded by these researchers that the Dow stocks actually showed lower rates of return on a daily basis. This means that the futures may pull the Dow stocks over a short period of time. It also means much more when it is considered how the event takes place.

When the stock market is open, the futures tend to keep pace with the movement of the stock, which makes sense. However, when the stock market closes, the Dow and S&P futures continue to trade on through the night into the following morning. This process is so far crooked that it is hard to believe that it can even be called legal by the Securities and Exchange Commission. Throughout the night, the futures can go up or down by several 100 points on the Dow, and it can occur on fairly light volume. This means that it does not take very much capital to move the futures, especially when margin is considered.

The study by Robbani and Bhuyan (2005) also shows that the trading of futures attracts uninformed people along with those who may be highly informed. In other words, all it takes is a spark by those who can exercise a capital commitment, and such action will activate whatever crowd there may be. It is true that the up or down move in the futures may occur just before the stock market opens with the release of an economic report, which is understandable. However, there is no excuse for the futures to make a big move without any public release of influential information. The only explanation is that an outside force with a specific intent acts on the futures for the sole purpose of taking the market either up or down at the open. Then, at the open, market makers can easily either distribute or accumulate stock inventory at prices that are either higher or lower than the prior market close.

We have a situation here where the futures actually influence the stock prices instead of the other way around. Once again, it is a world turned upside down for the advantage of the control establishment. If it were to be determined that stocks were being hoarded and that the supply of stock was going to be reduced, then that would be a valid reason for the futures to go through the roof. If corporate earnings and economic reports showed that the future was promising, then that would be a valid reason for the futures to go ahead of the general market. However, for the futures to somehow go through the roof or crash in overnight trading without any fundamental change in the price of stocks from the close of the market, then that should be cause for a federal investigation. Although this sort of event is to be considered legally crooked, it certainly borders on abuse and possibly criminal activity.

9

THE FINANCIAL MEDIA

People depend too much on what they see and hear, the material things in life. People tend to live solely by the five physical senses (sight, hearing, smell, taste, and touch). However, these senses can be used as a medium for deceit. In reality, the physical senses can be used as a weapon against those who live by them. The fact remains that people can be deceived in any one of these five senses.

Since the financial media (including wire services) is directly involved with sight and sound, it must be assumed that the media is a very potent weapon that can be used against the public. There is also a tendency amidst the public to accept news articles and releases as absolute fact. In general, the news media does an excellent job of reporting the facts and investigating for the truth, except when it comes to the economy and the stock market. It is therefore imperative for the investor to realize exactly how the financial news should relate to his diagnosis of the market.

Whenever a dictatorship takes control of any nation, the first order of business is always to take control of the visual and written media. The purpose of this is obvious. The people must always be brainwashed into believing the objective of the propaganda. In other words, people must be controlled into behaving in a certain way.

The news from the average daily review of the market appearing on the financial page could not be more misleading if it were purposely designed to fool the reader. The news, as seen in the newspaper, is quite often nothing more than just the authorized release by the news agency of the New York Stock Exchange. Any news release that has been authorized by the NYSE must never be accepted on the same level as an investigative report by a reputable newsperson not affiliated with any Wall Street establishment.

Any news releases that go through Dow Jones or the NYSE must be handled in a special way by the speculator. To use the word "suspicion" in describing the situation is putting it lightly. It may be worthwhile for you to know that it has been the policy of the NYSE to inform stock specialists of all relevant news releases before public release. If this does not concern you, then you deserve whatever they perpetrate upon you.

The NYSE can justify keeping the specialist informed before public release on the grounds that it is his job to keep the market orderly. Certainly, if the specialist was a neutral party, it would be difficult to argue with the concept. However, there have been too many cases of unusual occurrences just prior to a news release. Furthermore, all too often the blame of insider information is placed on people less guilty than the ones who operate the exchanges. This writer has witnessed too many cases where the specialist has accumulated, or distributed stock before the news release has taken effect. Then, to make matters worse, the specialist was given credit for saving the market. Despite the existence of the Securities and Exchange Commission, this practice continues, because there is nothing illegal about it according to the law. It is obvious that there are many things that can be considered immoral and yet be legal.

Always consider the motive that may be behind a released statement. Interpreting the news becomes a very important segment of your investment strategy. When you observe a press release from a major newswire company, you should determine if it is composed by the corporation that is involved, or you should observe if it is composed by a news release editor that merely paraphrased the original corporate release. When an original article is paraphrased, it means that someone else, an editor, for example, has used his own words to describe the original article. This can happen as a report on television or as a newswire release. When this happens, certain keywords can be inserted into the news that may not be found in the original press release. If the stock price plummets as a result of the news, then be watchful for follow-up activity. If the corporation and

61

market maker firm that is involved does not openly complain about any inaccuracies, then it means that there is most likely collusion with all of the parties involved. In other words, the market makers were most likely short the stock, and this means that others were also short the stock. The abuse which is possible in paraphrasing an original article can only be considered legally crooked. The investor should also analyze the headline.

When I first began dealing with the market, I would always become influenced by news articles featuring new product programs and future sales projections. I would immediately check the price, and each time, I would notice that the price was already up sharply. Many times, I noticed that the price had already been advancing either one or two days before the news release in "The Wall Street Journal." Emotion would then take over. As a result, I just had to get in before it was too late. Needless to say, the price would always go back down after a day or two of being on the active list. I finally learned from this that new product ideas by a company or even reports of good earnings will not produce profits for new buyers of the stock over the near term once the news is released. Emotional enthusiasm will only serve to destroy the speculator.

While a news article may imply higher corporate earnings as a result of a new product or business acquisition, it usually does not mention that fundamentals and market price are two different things. It may take years for a new product to earn a profit, while in the meantime, a downward cycle in the market may considerably lower the stock's price.

News articles dealing with economic matters should be met with even more suspicion. Whenever the news media concentrates on a particular economic problem, it is usually geared to make people do the wrong thing. The release of an economic report without the proper criticism that should go with it, represents a disservice to the public.

Economic statistics can be geared to appear positive or negative, depending on how the numbers are explained. For example, low economic activity could mean that interest rates will decrease (good), or it could mean that a recession is beginning (bad). Higher oil prices could mean inflation, but what if most other commodities are going lower? Perspective can be slanted in the media, depending on what economic element is being emphasized. Therefore, you should consider a contrary viewpoint in your diagnosis of the market. You may find, that during a bull market, exchange insiders are buying when the news is bad (slanted toward the negative).

When a news release involves a stock recommendation by a major brokerage house, your suspicion should once again be aroused. If you are a streetwise investor, you will immediately assume that the stock specialist has been informed of the announcement well before its release. Furthermore, an intelligent investor should immediately visualize the implications considering the source of the recommendation. After all, a brokerage house analyst is an employee of the brokerage firm, and therefore, such an analyst owes allegiance to the establishment which owes allegiance to the stock exchange. It can only be assumed that the public is the last to know about the contents of the news release.

A brokerage house recommendation, advertised through the news media, can mean that someone has taken advantage of lower prices and that someone now wants the public to focus on the stock. The key word here is "distribution." However, the situation is still subject to interpretation, because distribution can come in different ways.

It is most probable that the recommended stock will show strength over the very near term. Such a show of strength will get the brokerage "off the hook." The big blocks and heavier volume (distribution) will usually occur at higher prices in a short period of time. This would not necessarily mean that a long-term top is taking place. The distribution which would lead to lower prices could very well lead to another accumulation. Once that accumulation is accomplished, the brokerage would merely reaffirm the recommendation which would lead to a further advance. In such a situation, you could possibly withstand holding the stock for the longer term, but it would be a different story if holding stock options. Whatever the case, just be aware that the stock specialist will be supplying the market to accommodate the demand. When his inventory runs out, he will sell short.

The public makes more mistakes by following the financial news than for any other reason. This situation works out well for stock specialists and other smart money people. Since the smart money people can predict the behavior of the public and fund managers, news becomes a means for the smart money people to benefit. If you can exercise a reasonable amount of justified reasoning based on what has been presented here, you will be much better off. The news should not be neglected since it is an important element in your analysis. It can often be the key to your success. You should merely know how to handle it properly and be able to connect it to your method of diagnosis.

The TV stock market channels are observed by many people. Throughout the day, hundreds of presentations are made on the air. Many of these presentations deal with market outlook and opinion. Program directors can present whatever they wish. This means that they can present whatever someone else may wish who may be above them in authority. The link between a program director and a higher authority within the media firm will not end at that point. There will most likely be a link between the higher authority of the media company and the Wall Street establishment. That final link will not be inscribed in any company manual. It will simply be the personal interaction of upper management who may have favors to maintain with those who supply cash inflow to the media by way of advertising revenue. Without advertising revenue from the Wall Street establishment (the NYSE and major broker members), a TV business channel is nothing. This is a mutual benefit situation of critical proportions. They need each other. The media will sacrifice their own people for the sake of sponsor revenue.

In his book "The Wall Street Gang," Richard Ney stated that the ability of the NYSE to suppress the truth is due more to its control over the nation's media and the machinery of information than to economic power. Ney summarized the existence of the financial media by saying that so long as investors are persuaded to accept the teachings and rationalizations of the wire services, the hypnotic masterminds of the financial media will continue to control the decisions of investors. He was saying that wire services, radio, and television are all being used as tools to control investors under the control of exchange operators and management.

People cannot see the forest for the trees. In other words, investors get pointed by the media to bits and pieces of released information instead of visualizing the big picture. When a piece of targeted good news is released, people will jump with it. Then, investors crumble when a piece of bad news is released a few days later. Methods of this type propagated by the control establishment are what makes investors react for the purpose of benefiting establishment stock dealers. Observing those up and down reactions caused by economic reports should be proof enough that the scheme being perpetrated is legally crooked. It all becomes legal because the producers in the media know how to use words in such a way that it could never be proven to be deliberate lies. However, the truth remains that it is all crooked because it all converges to a point where it becomes easier to hide the truth than to reveal it. It becomes an act of nature, which is inherent in humans, where individuals will often find avenues of deceit to be more convenient than trying to stand on the rigors of the truth.

10

THE WRONG TIME TO BUY

The wrong time to buy is when price records are being broken; when newspapers are praising the particular stock or industry; when the company is being spotlighted; when brokerage analysts are recommending the stock; and most of all, when the majority of analysts are bullish. This section does not have to be overly loaded. The mentality is simple enough.

It is the wrong time to buy a stock when it meets with heavy volume after an extended rally. It is strongly the wrong time when a stock, which has been advancing, suddenly advances sharply on very heavy volume with many big blocks being traded. This means that the public is buying heavily as market operators are unloading stock.

While it may be good to buy on declines in a bull market, it can suddenly become the wrong time to buy in the early stages of a bear market. The height of bullishness occurs when a stock or the general market reaches a long-term top. There lies the problem. Investors continue to expect new highs to occur after a normal correction. On the second rise leading to a double top on the charts, brokerage dealers will short heavily against public buyers.

It is amazing how much buying is done by the public with the mutual funds on a decline after a stock has sold at a record high price. In other words, the specialist allows the price to drive upward without resistance and then sells heavily against the demand. He continues to supply stock as it declines while public buyers enter the market anticipating a mere reaction called "profit-taking."

At a long-term top, the specialist will short heavily. Once he acquires a heavy short position, he will want the stock to drop sharply. To ensure that the price does not rise with the incoming demand, he merely advises his special clients to unload their holdings, whether directly or through his brokerage network. The clout behind this action is tremendous. Once this process is in motion, support levels will not hold as they would have during a bull market.

There may be several support levels extending down from a high. It is not advisable to buy at the first line of support unless it happens to be the only line. While specialists may rally a little from the first support, its only purpose will be to unload inventory acquired on the decline. If it should be a temporary bear market, it will be wrong to buy unless a lower support level is reached.

Investors will always wonder if they should short when it seems that prices are high. Shorting is not advised in the traditional sense of the word. If investors short stock, it will show up as a short sale. The market makers will know where the short positions are located, and this is much like giving away your hand in a game of poker. Instead of actually shorting a stock, it may be advisable to acquire put options as an insurance hedge protecting your stock position. Of course, if the stock is not owned, the speculative strategy would be to acquire put options on the stock or on the S&P index. The important thing to remember is that if the market maker knows there is a heavy public short position located at some point, he will act to decimate those positions.

11

THE DISTRIBUTION STAGE

The general rule presented in this work is that volume increases steadily until record-breaking volume occurs at or near a major top. Therefore, the most dangerous time to be long is at that time when market averages are at the highest levels accompanied by extremely heavy volume.

A long-term major top is more likely to be accompanied by heavy volume. A series of intermediate tops may or may not be accompanied by heavier than usual volume. However, in those instances when heavy volume does occur after an extended rise, it certainly is valuable to know that a top is about ready to take place. If a top does occur on light volume, it is indicating it is not a major, long term top and that its price will advance again. Whatever the case, heavy volume must be feared by bulls and welcomed by bears going short.

While the public is buying heavily on the rally, the stock specialists and other market makers are both selling and taking a heavy short position. Of course, this is a major reason why the public is not very successful. At major turning points, the market maker does the opposite of the public.

If the public is buying on heavy volume, you should not buy but should consider selling instead if in an extended rally. It is a matter of the experienced versus the inexperienced, and the latter certainly outnumber the former many thousands to one. Knowing all this, do you really want to follow the crowd?

You must always remember that nothing is ever as good as it seems or as bad as it looks. Otherwise, it would be so easy to make money by just going along with the general mood or hysteria. For example, major distribution occurs when unemployment is low; when factory production is near capacity; when the media persists in reporting good news; and when the future seems to be assured of being even better.

You must remember that whenever the future seems certain, the opposite will usually occur. Whenever you get the feeling that public sentiment is very bullish and that a long position is assured of success, you must develop the discipline to resist the inclination to buy. Although these rules sound simple, it does require what most people do not possess. In essence, it requires a tenacious and emotionless character as far as the market is concerned.

On average, a specialist may have about ten to twenty stocks to maintain. However, he is certainly not going to treat his stocks alike. He will probably initiate distribution in the lower quality issues first and top out the higher quality stocks last. By distributing his stocks at different times, he can switch his resources from one issue to another. Therefore, at an important top, he may have about one-third of his stocks already declining with nearly two-thirds being in the process of distribution and with perhaps one or two stocks being geared to go higher.

Each stock must be evaluated individually in order to determine how its distribution period compares with the projected distribution of the general market. It is easy to see that the specialist must also maintain an operation of evaluation and coordination in order to maximize his resources. He certainly cannot do this on the floor of the exchange because of the velocity of the trading. Each specialist does have a team working for him. He is part of a firm which maintains employees. It is the job of these employees to keep the specialist informed and to coordinate the operation.

In order to keep investors bullish throughout a market top, specialists will always distribute the smaller and weaker stocks first and keep the stocks which compose market averages until the end. Of course, the advance-decline line will most often reveal this since there is a much broader range of stocks not in the Dow nor in the S&P averages. In other words, while the major averages may look strong, the majority of the secondary and lower level stocks may actually be trending downward. This may show prominently on the NYA index.

Ney (1970) emphasized the point that targeted short selling does stop advances, and short covering does cushion declines when done at the right times. While referring specifically to NYSE specialists, he meant that specialists have the power to make money on a continual basis by shorting against public buying with the use of financial credit. In other words, he was saying that a specialist can actually stop an advance by soaking up the buy orders. This, in itself, should be enough to anger any investor. The point to be made at this time becomes quite simple. Nothing has changed over time despite all the rhetoric contained in all of the new laws and regulations that may have been passed. Human nature remains constant, whether it be within the NYSE specialists or Nasdaq market makers.

In conclusion, the reader should realize that there will be many buyers for each seller at a top. This is why volume will increase. There will be many buyers from a smaller number of people who are selling large blocks. Furthermore, the supply of stock going to people that are jumping into the market may be coming from short sales by the brokerage. Therefore, it is wrong to assume that there is always one buyer for every seller. You must remember that it will be just a few brokers that will be selling to many buyers. At a top, there will be many buyers for every seller. The smaller number of sellers have more stock to rid and have more resources to short against every buyer. When the buyers run dry, the market turns, and other investors with long positions fuel the decline. The market is not an auction where one seller equals one buyer. For example, a seller of 1000 shares may be selling to two buyers at 500 shares each.

12

THE RIGHT TIME TO BUY

The best time to buy for the long-term is when nobody is saying anything about the stock; when it looks weak but refuses to go down in spite of heavy selling; when the news media ignores it; when people are bearish on it although the price seems to have formed a base. At that point, the odds are more in favor of accumulation rather than distribution by insiders. By reversing the public rule of buying on the way up, at the top and on the way down, you will realize a better chance of making a profit. Although the general market will allow this type of opportunity only once every several years, there are really many such opportunities in individual stocks throughout each year. Many of these are missed due to a lack of attention.

The right time to buy for the short-term while in a bull market is when a stock, which has been declining, drops sharply on heavy volume or encounters big block trades near a low. This would constitute accumulation by the stock specialist. However, personal judgment is required to determine if it is short or long-term accumulation. First, you should observe the block trades on the rally. If the institutional funds continue bullish on the reactionary rally, then you should expect a further decline with heavy volume at lower prices.

On any sharp drop which induces heavy volume, you should relate the occurrence with other market factors and the technical pattern on the price chart. It is more bullish when going to a major support level on heavy volume. There is more risk at higher support levels. At the reversal point, the specialist would absorb public selling by short covering, and then he could begin buying for his own account.

The best way to buy at a low point in a stock's trading range is to wait for a downside extreme on very heavy volume. You should also look for a cushion built into the stock's price, such as its book value or its price-earnings ratio. At that point, the specialist will be either heavily short covering or buying as the public is forced out. Many times, the specialist will rally the stock immediately off the low. However, the specialist will sometimes accumulate long positions on the second low with the first low acting as the short covering stage. Thus, a double bottom may form.

In order to buy at these low points, one must believe that heavy volume at a yearly low represents accumulation. There certainly should be no doubt in anyone's mind that such a condition will offer the best possible odds for the investor. It is better than waiting for a stock to break out of a trading range. This method of observing heavy volume will work out best with the high quality or the more volatile issues. The quality stocks will advance more quickly after an accumulation. The secondary issues are more likely to take a longer period of time in the accumulation stage.

How much volume will constitute accumulation leading to a reversal to the upside? Although there can be no set percentage increase in signifying the reversal, it is safe to say that it should be at least 100 percent over the average volume.

It may be a good idea to gauge the volume in relation to the quality of the stock. While a 100 to 200 percent increase in volume may be acceptable for a Dow stock, at least a 200 percent increase in volume may be more desirable for a high-quality secondary issue. A lower quality secondary stock may require well over a 300 percent increase on a daily basis average. While it may be more sophisticated to observe the big blocks on the tape, anyone is capable of looking up the volume figures in the newspaper.

Capitulation

Capitulation is a rare point in time which usually occurs at a major market bottom. It is important to understand because it is an event that is actually orchestrated by market makers and the brokerage establishment. It is that point in time when investors, even those that may have been bullish, finally give up and sell. The bulk of this capitulation may occur over two or three days until all those on margin are forced out with margin calls. Keep in mind that brokerage firms know exactly where the bulk of margin calls will kick out. While these brokerage firms may say they do not want their clients to get hit with margin calls, they do not tell you that the stock being given up by those clients will go directly into the accounts of the brokerage at bottom prices.

Quite often margin calls represent the best indicator when looking for a bottom. Since the specialists and other forms of market makers have a good idea of the price level that would initiate massive margin calls, he will strive to drop the price to that level. This process is fairly quick usually covering no more than three days. Once the margined shares are sold by investors, the price turns up as if by a miracle. Being fully on margin can be very dangerous when buying at high historical valuations. There is nothing wrong with margin so long as you do not allow yourself to be completely at the mercy of the system.

Just remember the simple rule of thumb concerning margin calls. When you hear of a heavy amount of margin calls being issued, you will know that it is the right time to buy. Margin calls are issued after the close, and action must usually be taken on the open of the following session. It is on such openings that a bottom is attained as market makers grab shares that must be given up by margined investors. As can be seen, the rules are geared in favor of the major brokerage firms. This is just another example of the system being legally crooked.

13

THE ACCUMULATION STAGE

The strength of a stock or the general market depends on the make-up of its foundation. It all depends on the amount of stock in strong hands. In other words, specialists, exchange insiders, and favored clients are always to be considered strong hands. As long as these people are holding, the market will be bullish for the longer term.

At a market top, the majority of the trading stock has shifted or is in the process of shifting from strong to weak hands. Of course, weak hands represent new holders who may be highly leveraged and mostly geared for short term speculation. Weak hands may also be institutional funds which are being operated by poor management. At this point, it must be mentioned here that the mutual funds are a blessing to the market makers. Because mutual and index funds by their nature have to be in the market at all times, the specialists will always have someone to hold the bag before the fall.

At a market bottom, there is a flow of stock from weak hands to strong hands. Of course, this process occurs over a period of several weeks. At the low point, there may be a lot of weak-hand selling and strong-hand buying which may be accompanied by a lot of short-selling by the weak hand faction. As the stronger element absorbs the stock, downside momentum declines and a foundation is formed. This occurs because the people who are able and willing to buy are in a more powerful position than those considering selling.

The smart money element will accumulate in the lower ranges through a slow process or in a short period of time during a climactic selloff on brisk volume. Remember that these concepts can apply to the general market as well as to the individual stocks. However, we must not mix apples and oranges. We have the general market to consider, and then we have the individual stocks. There will always be individual stocks that will either be topping off or forming bottoms despite whatever the general market may be doing.

After a bear market is eight to twelve months old, those who sell short or those who simply sell are of the less experienced type of speculators. There may be times, when during a bear market, a particular stock may be going to the high range. In these cases, such stock may be due for a short-term correction, but this comes under the heading of speculation.

The smart money element will begin buying before the market hits the bottom. Their method is to "buy undercover." Quite often, when specialists and other well-informed sources are accumulating, they do not bid as the public would do. They merely let other people offer their shares. The buyers may well contend that they are doing a favor to the sellers.

On such occasions, brokers often report to investors that little stock is wanted and that support is poor, concluding that the market is going lower. This sort of analysis does not take into account the buying that is going on under cover. When hitting a bear market bottom, the volume may actually dry up while the price resists further decline.

Accumulation during a bull market usually occurs with heavy volume and/or with big block trades at a low point in the trading range. The best clue that indicates this process is when the price resists decline despite the occurrence of any heavy volume.

Although a double bottom formation on the chart is not necessary for showing accumulation, it certainly does help to confirm the process. A double bottom or "W" formation usually occurs at a bear market bottom, but it can also occur well into a bull market within a trading range. The double bottom allows specialists to cover heavy short positions on the first low and then allows them to accumulate heavy long positions on the second low.

As far as individual stocks are concerned, a very bullish situation would be a reverse head-and-shoulders formation, a downward spike on extremely heavy volume, or an "M" formation with the second down leg going lower than the first representing the bulk of accumulation. The third leg down allows for more accumulation as investors now believe that the stock is going to a new low.

The situation at a bottom is just the opposite of when it is at a top. There may be many sellers for every buyer. A market maker could be buying from many sellers at a major bottom. It is for this reason that it is wrong to believe there is one seller for every buyer. This becomes part of the illusion that is propagated by the media. In reality, there is one trade which represents a buy and a sell. However, there could easily be one trader executing many buys with many investors. Therefore, stock market commentators are propagating the illusion of equality all the time by saying there is one buyer for every seller. This is just another example of being legally crooked.

14

WHEN STOCKS ARE MARKED UP

A stock specialist believes there is no sense in marking up a stock's price to a high level if he cannot get the public or the institutions to take his inventory off his hands at the high price. His purpose is to raise the value of his accumulation to a point where he can distribute on heavy public demand. The specialist knows there are many people that will only buy something when it is high in price. When something is cheap, it is not worthy of notice. This clearly shows the mentality of the public and the managers of public funds.

While marking up his price from a low, the stock specialist attracts a following, first from the floor traders and then from the institutional funds which help in his marking up operation. The operator will initiate the advance only when he feels that the stock will eventually attract broad public buying.

To understand why the specialist has control, the following should be considered. A stock specialist has access to confidential information since he has direct contact with corporate directors and is able to attend board meetings. Whether he attends the meetings or not, he keeps informed. Therefore, he knows when something new is being planned long before it hits the news media. He is also aware of the earnings report before the results are publicly released.

When a stock begins to move into a new range, it represents a long-term trend to the upside. This would indicate a technical breakout on the charts. The rise is usually destined to continue for several months. However, at certain points, there will be reactionary movements designed to induce investors to sell. The specialist can make much more money by selling on heavy volume rallies and buying on heavy volume declines during an extended bull market movement.

In the marking up process, the specialist makes good use of his two separate accounts. He maintains a trading account and a long-term account. With these two individual accounts, he is able to take advantage of tax laws and circumvent securities regulations. He will use his trading account for all short-term trading but will use his long-term account for long term capital gains when such a tax law is in effect. With two accounts, he can maneuver positions to his advantage.

Depending on the tax laws in effect, price charts clearly show that stock prices get marked upward just before a holding period is ready to end. Of course, the holding period extends from a point that has been recognized as an accumulation. For example, if a market low occurs in early January with a one year holding period in effect for tax benefits, then it can be reasoned that the specialist will liquidate the bulk of his long-term account in the following January. He will do all in his power to mark up prices just prior to his distribution objective.

In general, how can the specialist mark up prices? He simply does not supply shares to the demand. On light volume during a bull market, price has a tendency to rise. If it does not rise, he instigates the advance by buying the excess supply which is not difficult to do when volume is light.

If a speculator is to be successful, he must think like a specialist and acquire a professional attitude. The speculator must believe in his own methods while maintaining an awareness of all other opinions concerning market conditions. Most of all, he must not be deterred by traditionalists who contend that stock specialists have no control over prices.

15

VOLUME AND PRICE

There is a very pronounced relationship between trading volume and price movement. It is not enough to simply say that price movement is due to a difference between supply and demand. It is more important to learn why the imbalance has occurred and how it relates to the specialist and the public.

During periods when prices are at peak levels and fail to make further headway, the trading volume is quite often at a high level. The most critical situation is known as "blow-off" volume which is when record volume occurs accompanied by a lack of price movement.

A "blow-off" will often signal a long-term top. In such a case, prices do not advance, because there is heavy distribution from strong hands to weak hands. Therefore, it is reasonable to believe that when the market has had a sustained advance and then fails to make further progress in the face of considerably increased volume, the market has reached a peak, and shares are being distributed for an imminent decline.

The price-volume relationship near a bear market bottom is not as clearly defined as when at a peak. However, when prices refuse to break to new low levels after numerous efforts to drive lower, and all of this is accompanied by increased volume, then it is probable that an important advance is ready to begin. The increased volume is simply the accumulation of stock by strong hands from weak hands. While at the bottom, this process will sometimes occur in a climactic sell-off.

These observations will also apply in a general way to individual stocks. Studying the individual stocks which follow the market may give a better picture of what is happening. Of course, there are always some stocks that will go against the trend because of special circumstances. Many times, a stock will go against the general trend in the market, because it has not gone through accumulation or distribution.

Trading at Turning Points

Forget the notion that there is one buyer for every seller as told on the major media channels. At the top of a price movement, there may be one seller for many buyers, and at the bottom of a movement, there may be one buyer for many sellers. This concept should not tax any brain of average intelligence. At a top, there could be ten people buying 100 shares each and one entity selling 1000 shares. At the bottom, there could be ten people selling 100 shares each and one entity buying 1000 shares. Keep in mind that there are always more dumb people than smart people at major price turns. This is evidenced by the fact that bullish sentiment is strongest at market tops.

16

BIG BLOCK ACTIVITY

Sophisticated speculators should consider big block activity as a crucial indicator. In general, a big block trade, when a rally is underway, is to be considered negative since it may represent distribution by the specialist or other smart money entity. In reverse, a big trade on a decline can be considered positive since it may represent accumulation. Big block activity is concentrated at the top and bottom of short and long-term cycle trends. In other words, this type of activity provides the signal for a reversal of trend.

If market activity is slow, a block of 100,000 shares may be cause for alert in stocks like IBM or Intel, but at more active times, a block of 500,000 shares or more may be worthy of attention in a large capitalization issue. Certainly, a block of one million shares in a stock like IBM should always be cause for concern especially when the trade occurs first thing in the morning or as one of the last trades or after an extended advance or decline during the session.

On average, it is easier to buy a big block than it is to sell it as far as the investor is concerned. If you want to buy a big block, the specialist can look around for a seller or a group of sellers while edging the price up, or he can sell you the block from his inventory if he so desires. If you want to sell a big block, he can simply let the market slip until enough sellers make up the number of shares or until he finds the price tempting enough in which case you are at his mercy.

If you are ever in possession of a big block, you may want to consider breaking it up so that the market maker does not suspect that you are trying to unload a huge number of shares. Do a little at a time throughout the session. The commission cost may not be that great.

Laying a big block on the line may cause the price to decline before much of it is sold. This writer has experienced such market behavior. Never alert the dealers as to what you plan to do. Selling stock, as with anything else, is always more difficult unless the activity is very brisk.

If you ask your broker concerning your block of stock, he will often say that you will get a better price if you sell the whole block together. On the NASDAQ, the order will be given special handling while trying to find a dealer to buy. However, during this process, dealers will be alerted as to the size of your block and the price that you are asking.

Everyone loves a buyer. It is almost always easier to buy a big block than to sell. The problem is that you may not get the low price of your initial order. If you are sitting there at the bid trying to buy a large block, you may find the price going up before you ever get confirmation.

It may be worthwhile to apply these same rules when dealing with stock options. Even if you are going at the ask to buy or at the bid to sell, a dealer is only required to buy or sell a certain number before changing the price. The same holds true for stock.

Since the average investor may not deal with large blocks, let us consider the activity of big blocks by others. Consider the case of a quality stock which is in a major bullish trend. Such a stock could very well fall into a decline (correction) within a bullish trend. This will occur right after distribution by a specialist and/or other big concern within the institutional establishment. When such correction occurs, a speculator must determine where to buy. This facet of the game is the most interesting part of the market. As a matter of fact, it is the most important part of the game.

Even a Dow stock may continue to slide while the Dow advances. When this occurs, the smart speculator should immediately take note of the situation. Patient observation will be required.

As the stock goes lower on fairly light volume, many people will make the horrible mistake of buying it. Once a correction cycle has begun, do not buy the stock if it shows light volume. It is totally against the odds to buy with the momentum on the downside and without any evidence of accumulation.

There are two ways to enter a stock that has been declining. One way is to wait for the price to form an upward reversal in trend. However, the best way is to look for a substantial increase in big block trades.

The ideal situation is when big blocks of ten thousand shares or more cross the tape at a specific price level. As the blocks cross the tape, the price should hold steady as it forms a base. Sometimes this process only takes minutes before the price begins to rise. However, in the ideal situation, it may take one whole trading session. Some of the high-volume stocks may even take up to two sessions. A more volatile issue may take no more than one hour.

Big block activity at a correction low is not just a matter of chance. At that point, which is often considered by traditionalists as a technical support level, is really that point where there are massive sell stops known by the specialist.

In the ideal situation, a stock will form a top on higher than normal volume. These situations are easy to spot. However, there are many times when a stock will top on average volume. If you are suspicious that a top may be forming on average volume, you should check to see if any large blocks have traded. Unless you subscribe to a quote service, you can always call your brokerage and ask the broker to look up any large blocks that may have traded. He will be able to read those off his computer screen with the amount traded along with the price and time.

A specialist will gladly top off a stock or form a bottom on fairly low volume if he can transact a big block. In order to observe this sort of evidence, a more sophisticated speculator should employ a quote service through his computer that will list the actual trades by volume as they occur.

Once you know the size of the trade, the price and the time it occurred, you will have all the tools necessary to carry out this work properly on your own.

17

BLOCK-VOLUME REVERSAL

The basis for belief in block-volume reversal is really more than just theory. It is very real and accepted by professionals in the industry. It is considered a theory only by those people who do not comprehend that the stock market is much more than just an ordinary auction. Heavy volume and the trading of big blocks of stock are the most significant factors in the analysis of individual stocks and the general market along with basic technical analysis (charting).

Although block-volume reversal is so easy to understand and so logical in nature, almost every investor does not abide by it nor place much importance on it. It is amazing that investors may witness an event, and yet, they may hardly take note of what their eyes have seen. It is a lack of registration on the brain when sight cannot see what it has not been prepared to see. An illusion of strength or weakness can easily deceive all those who are not prepared.

People have witnessed for decades that volume tends to increase at cycle tops and bottoms and/or that big blocks of stock tend to trade more consistently at tops or bottoms. In practice, investors never seem to notice the importance of big blocks or heavy trading volume. There is always a tendency for people to buy stocks that have advanced and appear on the most active list. There is also a tendency for people to sell on a heavy-volume climactic sell-off.

Perhaps, the most difficult thing to understand in this type of analysis is the relationship between big block trading and volume. While most investors do notice changes in volume (although not realizing the importance of it), they hardly ever notice big block trades. Of course, the reason for this is simple. While volume figures may be published in newspapers, big block trades on the individual stocks are not. Big blocks go by unnoticed unless one is watching the tape or employs an appropriate quote service. Most investors do not subscribe to block reporting services.

Using volume alone in this analysis can produce satisfactory results, and certainly, an average investor is capable of using this basic system. However, taking big blocks into account does make the system much more sophisticated. Furthermore, an analyst must have a feel for the proper interpretation of the big blocks that have traded. It does take professional judgment that can only come from experience.

One must know exactly what is a big block. Is it 10,000 shares, 100,000 shares or more? In some of the smaller issues, ten thousand shares may be considered big. However, it may be better to relate the size of the block with the overall situation in the market. Big block trading can be considered in progress when a series of blocks occur at ten thousand shares and over. For example, a series of five 10,000 share blocks and four 50,000 share blocks is really equal to one block of 250,000 shares. If all those shares are going to the specialist, there would now be an accumulation of a very large block.

In trying to determine a long-term bottom, you would have to see many blocks of ten to fifty thousand shares plus several of 100,000 shares or over. For example, if a big Dow stock begins to decline several points, you should not buy into it until you see big block activity involving ten to fifty thousand share blocks along with some 100,000 share blocks. Only then should you speculate that you are very near a bottom.

Under a capital gains tax law, distribution takes longer to accomplish by stock specialists, because they have to hold stock in their investment accounts for at least the stipulated amount of time according to current tax law in order to be taxed at a lower rate. Under a six-month long-term capital gains law, stocks did usually reach a high about six months from the accumulation point. When the law was changed to the one-year holding period, stocks did reach a high one year from an important market low.

The market has to be held up to give enough time for exchange insiders to unload stock in order to receive long term tax benefits coupled with maximum profits. Not all specialists accumulate and distribute at the same time, and so the distribution periods will vary for each stock. When the market is making a major top, the distribution will often have to be stretched over several months.

When the tax holding period is greater than one year, we may have a problem. There will most likely be less incentive for specialists to keep a freeze on capital for a long period of time just to get a break on taxes. They can make so much more money by working it over the short term and merely pay a little more in taxes.

If stock specialists have no incentive to hold stock for a long period of time, heavy distribution and accumulation can occur much more quickly throughout the market. Extremely heavy volume will be much more significant. As a result, market reversals will occur more abruptly. The various specialists will have no incentive to hold for long periods because too many things can change in the economic scene. Specialists will have more incentive to create very wide price swings, adding more volatility to the market.

Because tax laws do change, it is important for the investor to keep informed on the tax laws regarding the holding period of stock for long term capital gains. The tax situation will be more relevant with heavy positions.

Extremely heavy big block trading (specialist short selling) will occur at bull market tops. While the process may be more prolonged and widespread at major tops, it is more concentrated at major bottoms.

At a bear market low, overall volume quite often contracts as sellers run out. Although volume may be low, all big block trades will be of critical importance. It will be then that big blocks and low volume work together. Block-volume reversals do not occur only at major tops and bottoms. There can be many short-term block-volume reversals in a stock within one year. This is because a stock specialist will accumulate and distribute a specific stock many times within a bull or bear market.

Usually, heavy volume at a top is accompanied by big block trading. However, care must be taken to recognize that both are occurring at the same time. For example, if a stock forms what seems to be a bottom on heavy volume without the occurrence of an acceptable number of big blocks, then that particular bottom may hold only for the short term. In such a case, one must not consider the reversal to be of a major consequence. Big blocks and volume should go together. Although both are important, big block trades tend to carry more value.

If an issue drops to a low on light volume accompanied by just a few very big blocks, then this type of action may be bullish for the long term but not necessarily for the very short term. In many secondary issues, accumulation can occur over a period of months with very big blocks occurring at the lows every few weeks but accompanied with slightly increased volume. This type of process is to be considered a long-term reversal. Patience is required when buying into this situation.

The following two axioms support block-volume reversal analysis:

1. Under distribution, a specialist is able to supply big blocks of stock to any buyer, and a specialist will sell to many buyers.
2. Under accumulation, a specialist is able to buy big blocks of stock from any seller, and a specialist will buy from many sellers.

It is easy to see that under these conditions there is not always one individual buyer for every individual seller and vice versa. It is not correct to say that there is one bullish person for every bearish person and imply that the number of bulls and bears are equal for any number of trades.

When distribution is occurring, there may be thirty buyers for every seller. However, the sellers are selling off big blocks that were accumulated at lower prices and are perhaps breaking up larger blocks into smaller segments to supply the demand.

When accumulation is occurring, there may be one buyer for every twenty sellers. However, the buyers are now covering short positions which soaks up much of the selling, and they are also buying big blocks along with many smaller blocks from many individuals.

Heavy volume at the start of an advance can be considered bullish. However, it is more bullish to have lighter volume as the advance continues although traditionalists think the opposite. Once the advance has continued on lighter volume, the situation should be considered bullish until the volume increases suddenly well above an average amount into the upper volume range. A volume reversal will not usually occur on light volume. Therefore, the odds are good that the market will not reverse in any major fashion as long as light volume persists once an advance is underway.

When big block activity occurs on light volume during an uptrend, it means that the odds are good for a very short-term correction which will allow the specialist to purchase more inventory at slightly lower prices.

Although big block trading and heavy volume do signify a reversal, the reversal itself, in terms of price, may not necessarily occur on the same day. However, the block-volume reversal actually becomes reality even before prices begin to retract from the trend. Once the poison is injected into the system, it becomes a matter of time before the major averages reverse although not evident at first. There are cases where price begins to reverse amidst the heavy volume, and there are cases where price reverses on the first sign of decreasing volume from a record volume day.

When, in your opinion, the volume has increased substantially well into a rally, you must decide whether to sell immediately or to hold until the first sign of deterioration occurs. It is perhaps more difficult to sell with a profit than it is to buy into a position. It is also easier to buy on a rally than it is to sell. To be a true professional, you must sell to people who are finding it easy to buy.

There is no excuse for disregarding the danger signals during an advance. Heavy volume should serve as an alert. Big block trading merely confirms the alert. Once all of this occurs, you must observe carefully price behavior. For example, if the price continues to tick higher after each big block trade while going to new highs or cycle highs, then this type of activity should not be considered short selling by the specialist. It may simply signify that the specialist is supplying inventory to the market in a normal fashion. However, as his inventory runs out, he must turn to short selling to supply the market.

It is specialist short selling which is of critical importance. Significant specialist short selling is when big block trades occur at a specific price level without much price movement. At that point, the specialist will absorb all demand and prevent the price from rising. Then, as the price declines, he will cover short positions by purchasing big blocks. Finally, he will pick a certain price level in which to acquire long positions. These points which have just been presented are of primary importance.

In choosing your buying and selling point, you must first decide if you are striving for professionalism or merely wish to have fun behaving like a rank amateur. A rank amateur, of course, is one who is ruled by emotion instead of faith in a specific philosophy or discipline.

As with anything that requires interpretation and judgment, the mentality of the analyst is crucial. He or she must rely on experience and on the sixth sense (ability to draw from the subconscious).

Traditional philosophy says that volume precedes price. Without clarification, this traditional piece of wisdom is pure hogwash. Heavy volume at a bottom does precede price. However, once an advance is underway, it is the advancing price that creates more demand for the stock. It would be smarter to say that heavy volume precedes price reversal. Yes, heavy volume can be considered positive during the early stages of an advance, but it is not positive during the later stage. It is the increase in price that eventually causes volume to increase to an extreme.

Events at the Open and Close

The open and the close are important in signifying reversals. Both are equally important for different reasons. A specialist can exercise more authority on the open and close. He has the ability and authority to exercise massive power on the open especially when there is an imbalance in buy and sell orders.

The closing trades are often important in telling what the specialist is planning. Many abnormal things occur in the last minute of trading. During this time period, extremely big blocks will often be transacted. Quite often, the closing trades go unnoticed, because they appear on the tape after the close. These big block trades involving one hundred thousand shares and over are indicative of a near term reversal. The investor must determine whether the block was a purchase or short sale. It is most probable that a closing big block represents a specialist short sale.

Long term reversals will often occur at the very close of the market when the price is at yearly or record highs. The reverse may also be true at bottoms. At these reversal points, the specialist or any other market maker will get the chance to acquire a very large position in the direction that the market maker now wants to go. There have been cases where IBM actually traded a very huge block of shares after the close at the very peak of a bull market which represented a specialist short sale with the stock going to a mutual fund. When the specialist does not have the stock, he will merely short sell it in order to create the stock.

Institutional traders place importance on closing prices, and of course, net asset values of mutual funds are marked according to the closing price (Cushing and Madhavan, 2000). In the market, it is the nature of mutual funds to direct large blocks of stock to trade at the close in a "mark to close" basis. The market maker knows this very well. It is unfortunate that so many mutual fund managers are so ignorant. The rest is history.

It is the opening hour that becomes critical when a major reversal is set to occur. Extremely heavy volume on the open represents panic selling by the managers of public funds (mutual and pension). These people who trade on the open are merely reacting to the events of the prior session. It is this sort of behavior that allows the specialist to acquire a contrary position just before a reversal.

91

In conclusion, big block trades at the open or close to the open are worthy of serious consideration. A big block at the close is most probably a short sale by the specialist if done near the highs of the day. Big blocks to the upside at the open can only be construed as specialist short sales, although some of these trades can actually be the matching of institutional traders. However, extremely big blocks on the downside at the open must be considered to be either short covering or purchasing by the specialist. Whether or not this activity is geared for the long term depends on your judgment concerning the periods of accumulation and distribution. If the market is between periods, the block trades are most likely very short term in nature, because these big block positions can be dispatched easily on a daily basis by the specialist with a profit. The reader should realize that all of the mentioned issues in the present work can be combined into the final analysis.

18

UPSIDE VOLATILITY

Upside volatility accompanied by an overall pessimism amongst analysts and the public gives rise to a situation which is an exception to the general rules of block-volume reversal. This process is sometimes known as "climbing a wall of worry."

Although it is rare, there are times during a bull market when stock prices go beyond an already overbought situation. When this occurs, the public continues to short sell heavily in anticipation of a correction. During this type of advance, volume can increase substantially accompanied by an obvious increase in big block trades. Under these conditions of upside pressure, big blocks of stock must be treated with a different type of judgment.

Many of the big blocks that occur on a continual rise are exchanges between institutional funds. The purchaser of a big block has to reach upward to a point where there is a big block sell order. This behavior helps to raise the overall trading momentum. Of course, since the market does gyrate throughout the day, the specialist and the Nasdaq market maker can always short sell toward the end of a rally and then cover short positions on any drop on a daily basis. This can all be done within one session.

Specialists are able to buy and sell big blocks of stock with profitable results while going through a sustained volatile upside move. Under these conditions, they will initiate sudden price movements within the session. For example, the Dow may go through an up and down movement of thirty or forty points within minutes which allows the specialist to cover big block short positions. Then by purchasing more inventory, they can rally the market back in a short period of time.

As long as the big block trades occur at varying price levels, you can be reasonably sure that a major reversal of the trend will not occur. The easiest way to detect a reversal is when a group of big blocks is concentrated in a tight price range. Another way to detect a reversal in a volatile market is when the overall volume approaches a record-breaking level. These types of reversals are not necessarily major bull market tops. Sharp and short declines are usually geared for specialist and other insider accumulation whenever the market has gone through a sharp advance within the context of a bull market.

Although some volatile advances can extend for several weeks, eventually they will transform into a corrective trading range. It is this trading range that allows specialists and favored clients to accumulate long positions in preparation for another advance. Quite often, this accumulation is accomplished with two or three downward moves to a support level on heavy volume.

19

SHORT SELLING ON DECLINES

A more advanced portion of specialist analysis involves short selling by specialists as the market declines from a major top. This concept may be difficult to accept given all else that has been said about big block trading. However, it is definitely worthwhile for the reader to reflect upon the following passages.

The tendency to buy on declines, after reaching a record top, represents another virtue of public weakness. Perhaps the most important marketing of stock by a specialist and other smart money people is done on the way down. Once the stock has reached an objective, the specialist is able to decline the stock by either selling stock or short selling. This process will absorb the demand and will provide profits for the operator.

Consider the following: It is amazing how much public buying is done on a decline after a stock has sold at a record high price. After having sold long positions followed by short selling, the specialist continues to supply stock as it declines while public buyers and fund managers enter the market anticipating a mere reaction called "profit-taking." Buying on such declines becomes most dangerous as a bull market gets older or as it enters the early stages of a bear market.

On these declines, big block trades may occur accompanied by only average volume. These big blocks do not represent specialist accumulation (block-volume reversal) if under certain conditions as follows: 1. if within a short time of having reached a new high; 2. if within about a 5% drop in a high price issue or a 15% drop in a low price issue; 3. if the price continues to drop after a big block has traded; 4. if on fairly low to moderate volume; 5. if during a small market rally; 6. if not at a recognized support level.

Quite often on charts, it can easily be seen that volume is highest on the day that the price takes the greatest tumble. This can happen on the day after the high is reached, or it can be several days after the high is attained. Big block trades may be evident on the initial decline.

The problem is to not mistaken these big blocks for an accumulation process (specialist short covering and buying). It will take a keen sense of judgment to determine the true situation. Although there may be various approaches to analyze big blocks, one possible method is to observe what happens after a series of big blocks.

If the blocks were short sales, the price would most likely go lower on the following day or perhaps on the same day. If the blocks were short covering or accumulation, the price should hold steady for a longer period of time with a steady flow of big blocks. If the price rises right after a series of big blocks, it would most probably signify a short rally only.

When institutions are buying big blocks on the way down with many at support levels, the specialist will receive these buy orders to be executed at designated prices. This means that he knows where all the buy orders are located. To avoid any new advance, the specialist will short against any big block buy orders and absorb demand. In the process, he can drive a stock right through a technical support level. This sort of situation will occur if the overall volume is low because it is easier for the specialist to sell and sell short without going to excess on low volume.

This pattern of short selling will continue until the price reaches an objective level at which the specialist knows that many sell stops are located. At the objective level, the specialist can very quickly cover his short positions and then commence acquiring long positions as the sell stops are processed.

The specialist will always want to stage a rally even though he wants the price to eventually go lower. Blocks of 100,000 shares or over after several days of decline may well mean that the specialist has accumulated just enough stock to retrace the decline 24 to 50 percent. There will always be people around ready to commit funds to this type of rally which eventually ends with more big blocks (specialist short sales). Specialist shorting in a bear market with optimistic fund managers guarantees the success of the specialist system.

20

MARKET MAKER ACTIVITIES
AND SPECIAL SITUATIONS

Knowing about the mentality and motivations of those who make the market must be considered as important as any of the most popular indicators constantly being reported by the media. Intelligent are those who do believe that market makers possess both direct and indirect power. It is unfortunate that the majority of people who realize this fact are themselves in the business of making the market. It is simply a fact of life that not many public investors really know anything about the securities business. The basic fundamentals of the stock market become meaningless if one does not know anything about the driving force within the market. Those who operate the market do know the mentality and motivations of those who invest, which is greed and fear. However, those who invest do not realize that those who make the market for the big brokerage houses possess the mentality and motivations of placing their firm's prosperity as well as their own before that of the investor. In other words, they make big money for themselves and sometimes make it look good by giving out some crumbs to the investor.

Overall, the basic operation involves getting investors to behave according to the desires of the market makers and the major brokerage houses. This devious behavior can always be justified by those public investors that win as a result. Those investors that lose as a result are simply branded "fools" and those who lose money would rather not admit to such, and so the system works rather well for those who operate the stock market casino.

Let us now look at some of the activities and special situations within the market. Let us also look at the required mentality of those who must operate in the market. Keep in mind that this writer is not saying outright that the system should be changed. This writer is saying that the investor should be better educated concerning the real world of those who operate the market. Market makers have to justify their existence.

REVELATIONS OF THE BROKERAGE BUSINESS

Let it be quite clear from the start that this writer has no argument against the individual brokers who work hard to help their clients prosper. I have known many brokers who possess the ultimate in ethics and integrity. The investor and the fund managers should lend their business to such independent brokers who take pride and satisfaction in their work. The argument here is against the major Wall Street brokerage houses that are integrated into the exchange insider establishment.

The problem has become so complex and so integrated into the brokerage system that the problem itself has become accepted by the government as well as by the public. However, this writer sees no problem in clearing this matter to very simple terms. The fact is that the big-time brokerage business is but one step away from the status of organized crime. In simple terms, it is legalized crime. Anyone reading the full contents of this work should know exactly what is meant by "legalized crime." Legalized crime is an activity that is considered illegal for the general public but not for a chosen few in authority within the industry, and that can easily be classified as unethical and immoral but is protected by a lack of law within the regulatory structure of the industry.

When I first became captured by the lore of the market at the age of twenty-one, I truly believed that all those who interacted with the investing public were to be respected as masters of market intelligence and possessors of the highest possible integrity. I wanted to be a broker so that I could enjoy the highest level of respectability. I truly believed that the bond between client and broker was like that of a patient and doctor. Well, the experience of slings and arrows soon shattered the fantasy.

I still recall walking into a branch of a major brokerage firm applying for a job. Being well educated in economics and business with an ability for analysis, I thought I could do well for investors. However, the floor manager soon set me straight about the real world of the brokerage business. He said outright to me that what he was looking for was someone he could approach with 100,000 shares of overloaded inventory and get rid of it all in one morning over the phone. I found out then and there that the client comes second and the brokerage comes first.

A little later in life, I did get a securities license in order to learn more about the business. The exam itself gave a clear indication of this business. In order to pass the exam, one needed only to know about legalities and a whole lot about stock options. There was nothing in the exam about stock analysis, or how to make money for the client. It all involved the protection of the brokerage business.

I was then exposed to telemarketing. In this stage of the game, the rookie broker is pressured into calling prospective investors from six in the morning to six at night. Throughout all that time, I heard of only one question being asked of people. How much did you make? It was never, how much did you make for your clients.

While in this position, I continually witnessed shares of stock (inventory) being unloaded over the phone by brokers who had no idea what they were really selling. The managers would even advise us not to buy what they were selling.

The firm with which I worked was a market maker. The brokerage itself carried an inventory which had to be retailed. The inventory would be accumulated by various means. The firm would buy on market declines and would also buy huge amounts of stock from other brokerage houses at wholesale prices. The point to make here is that not many investors realize that their brokers may have the capability of distributing stock inventory and that may be the reason why they may be getting calls to buy a firm's recommended issue. In other words, once a brokerage house has an overload of stock in a particular issue, it will issue an upgrade on that stock with a recommendation to buy.

One day, one of the sales brokers who knew I had an ability for analysis, asked me for an opinion on a stock that was being pushed for two dollars per share. When I told him that the book value was one cent per share, he scratched his head and said, "You mean there's nothing there?" I responded by saying, "There never was and never will be." At this point, we knew very well that this was nothing but legalized crime sanctioned by the NASD. Over the next several days, I cleaned out my records and files and left.

The name of the game is sales. The stock specialist is a merchant with inventory to sell. He buys at wholesale and sells at retail. That is the objective of the market maker. In order to accomplish this objective, the investor is required to buy at retail and sell at wholesale. In a bull market, there is room for both sides to win, but in a bear market, there is only room for the market maker to win.

Most depressing of all were conversations I witnessed between market makers. These people have no respect for investors. They believe that investors are like sheep that can easily be steered by trained salespeople. Furthermore, they do not really care about the product once it is sold and further believe that the same buyers will buy even more although the initial investment never appreciated in value. In other words, they believe that the public's addiction to greed will always keep them hooked. This has been proven. They can slap shareholders with unjustified downgrades over and over again and never lose a customer. Investors do not complain, and out of greed, they come back for more.

SHORTING TO INSIDERS

During an ongoing bull market, a rather unusual thing may occur during declines. There will always be a need for insiders to sell positions that have been maximized and to enter new positions. This type of accumulation involves huge amounts of stock which could never be accumulated in the small amount of time which occurs at the exact low. The specialist will actually short huge amounts of stock to exchange insiders. Using this method, he is able to fully supply the needs of all his private clients and make money on any little decline.

Needless to say, this is a very bullish situation. Since he is supplying insiders, he is not going to allow the stock to decline any great amount. Furthermore, he will cover his short position much quicker and thereby support the price.

One must look for evidence of this activity during an ongoing bull market. Once it is detected, one can be assured that the market has further to advance. In order to detect this type of activity, one must observe certain stocks day after day during the process of an advance and then on any ensuing decline.

Big block trades may occur during a rally with more big block trades during a short decline. The market may very well form a roller-coaster pattern either upward or to the downside. No matter what, there is an understanding between the specialist and the insider client. The process works well because while the insider is longer-term oriented, the specialist is very short term targeted.

This process of shorting to insiders will occur well off an established high but also just above a planned low. Very large blocks will begin to occur on small rallies. It should be obvious that these large blocks do not represent distribution since the market is well off its highs. Furthermore, these trades cannot possibly represent specialist accumulations since specialists would only accumulate on declines. Therefore, these should be recognized as short sales by specialists with the stock going to favored clients. Then on any declines, huge blocks of stock are seen traded which would then represent the specialist covering the short position by buying back the stock. The process can then be repeated with further shorting to insider accounts. Since these insiders are not buying at the lows, it must be with the understanding that the stock in question will be taken much higher by the specialist eventually.

After several weeks, a pattern begins to form as the market goes sideways to possibly a little lower. The large blocks which eventually amount to a rather considerable total can only mean that the market is destined to go much higher. In other words, these favored clients will eventually be able to unload that stock easily on heavy public demand.

BULLISH-BEARISH SCENARIOS

When the market advances early in the day and holds throughout the day with a sharp decline at the close, it means that specialists were giving investors plenty of time to buy with not much time to sell. During this time in which the market was up, specialists may very well have been shorting. Therefore, this is a bearish situation, because specialists are trying to delay investor selling until much lower levels are reached.

When the market stays on the negative side throughout most of the session with a sharp advance at the close, it means that specialists wanted to keep investors out of the market until a further advance takes place. This is a bullish situation because market makers spent most of the day accumulating as investors sold. It is also bullish because investors will now be buying well into the advance to help fuel it to higher levels.

Quite often an advance at the open is bearish because specialists love to short into these sharp rallies. As soon as the initial buying is over, prices usually drop. The scenario will vary. In a bull market, specialists may cover shorts into the second or third hour. In a bear market, an early morning advance may well be a cycle high which could lead to a long-term decline.

The reverse is true of a deep decline at the open. When the market collapses at the open, investors usually panic within fifteen minutes. Such declines are usually bullish since specialists are able to buy huge blocks of stock at lower prices. If one must sell on such a day, the sell should be entered on the ensuing rally after the first few minutes.

Emphasis must be placed on the fact that the first and last hour of each session is critical. However, more important in our analysis is the first and last few minutes of each session. There is so much more impact on investors within these boundaries than at any other time during the trading session. This will hold true even if trading hours are extended.

The first and last thirty minutes of each session are the most important to watch. Most bottom reversals occur within the first thirty minutes on a selling frenzy. The last thirty minutes are reserved for either upside or downside confirmation. Although this particular information is most applicable for the general market, it can be applied to individual stocks.

You can learn much about a specialist by observing the price movement of a specific issue over a long period of time. My favorite is the IBM specialist. The IBM specialists are true masters of the trade. With five minutes left to trade, I once observed the price taken down over one point on extremely small trades right up to the close. However, the final trade was a block of 100,000 shares. The following morning IBM opened up over one point and continued to advance over the longer term.

There is a point of ethics involved here. What about those people who got their stock sold out on stops at the close? Those people lost their stock and never got to enjoy the advance of the following morning. I am willing to bet that those investors never realized that they got scammed by the specialist. Of course, it is logical that people do not complain because they lack education on how the stock specialist system operates. This is just another example of legalized crime which would be illegal for an outsider to do, but it is perfectly legal for the market maker to do.

Of course, the NYSE contends that a specialist has a right to scalp stock or make a deal for shares at certain times. This implies that the deal for stock is rather minor. The question here becomes whether or not 100,000 shares of IBM is a minor situation. Furthermore, those investors that lost several thousand shares on a manipulated decline may not consider it such a minor event.

Quite often, a specialist will hold an order to execute at the close or possibly after the close. In the situation just described, someone had placed an order to sell at the close a block of 100,000 shares. The IBM specialist knew very well that he could not find a buyer to match the sale and that he would have to perform his duty to buy. Since he knew that the stock was going to advance, he gladly assumed the role of the buyer. At the close, he allowed the price to sink so that he could make the extra point. Since not many people are keen on my theory of specialist analysis, the whole act of acquiring this block seemed quite normal.

These events occur all the time and go unnoticed. They go unnoticed by investors and brokers alike because investors have not been introduced to the material found in this book. Market operators are successful in these maneuvers because no one complains. One cannot see the illusion for what it is if one does not suspect it is taking place nor realizes how it can take place.

At one time, I was watching Black & Decker very closely. It was trading in the teens. Over a period of thirty minutes, the BDR specialist accomplished a great feat. I noticed the price began to slip on light volume. It declined by two points in a very steady manner tick by tick. There was nothing radical about the movement. There were no big blocks being traded. Then something remarkable occurred at the very low of the day. I saw two blocks of 400,000 shares each go across at the very low. Once the last block traversed the tape, it began to advance and never went back. Who do you think bought those blocks? By the close, those two blocks were worth over one million dollars more than when the trade occurred.

Orders to be executed at the close can be either buy or sell orders, although sells may be more common since people on margin calls may have to liquidate by the close. Although there may be no problem with a small number of shares, a very large block should never be left to the mercy of a specialist or dealer. However, if you are a short-term trader, it would be worthwhile for you to recognize these occurrences. If the big block trade occurs with enough time for you to act, you may still be able to get your order in before the close after seeing the scenario mentioned here. Of course, if you are the one having to sell, avoid a sell order at the close. Even if you have a small block to sell, you may be grouped together with others in the same situation, in which case the total shares could very well make up a huge block.

The specialist or NASDAQ dealer can always justify a decline at the close by saying that there was very light demand for the shares. He would merely allow the price to decline before stepping in to buy for his own account. Once again, the dealer has the advantage.

Undermining Support

Specialists employ a very effective technique when they desire to take the market lower. It can simply be called "undermining support" for the lack of a better name. In basic form, it is a small decline or series of small declines each with a comeback to initial levels geared to clean the books of sell orders in preparation for a very sharp and substantial decline to much lower levels.

The best way to observe this process is through the movement of the Dow. If over a period of several days the Dow goes down and retraces back up to starting levels, it most likely means that specialists are executing all of the buy and sell orders that exist just under the market. The reasoning is that once the market does decline, in a deeper sense it will be a sharp decline which will not give investors much time to sell until the main decline is over. As the market declines over the area of prior declines, there will be hardly any buy orders to slow the decline or sell stops for the specialist to buy. This method can be used for both upside and downside movements. In other words, the specialist could rally several times to the upside and retreat which may turn investors negative. However, in reality, the specialist has merely cleared the way for a breakout advance by cleaning the area of major sell orders. Thus, resistance to the upside has weakened.

This undermining of support or cleaning the books process could take several sessions. It could be observed as a series of several sessions in which the market goes down substantially one day and up sharply the next day and so forth for a certain period of time either one week or possibly several weeks. It would show up on the chart as a sideways movement with equalized lines composed of 200 to 400-point movements over a period of up to three weeks. Under these conditions, the odds are good that the nearby support level will be broken. It would be wise to make preparation for a buying opportunity at the next lower support level if the market is considered to be in a general bull phase.

Activities at the Open and Close

Market makers are experienced concerning the process that investors and mutual funds perform. Just about every day there will be stocks that will have the designation of "sell or buy on the close." Of course, some will be designated as "sell or buy on the open." These trade situations may represent accounts that are on margin and margin calls have run out of time. Consider these situations carefully! Remember that the whole purpose of this book is simply to present rules of mentality so that the reader can reason out possible outcomes. Nothing is set in stone here. We are talking about human nature as it relates to the brokerage system.

First, let us consider the situation when the stock closes right at the low of the day. Those big trades that occur right after the close are the buy or sell orders at the close. Those orders are matched ahead of time. This has implications. If it is a big block sell at the close at the lows of the day, it could very well mean that it is a forced sale of a margined long position, or it could be a party that must sell by the close because that capital is needed for some other purpose. Either way, the market maker knows that it is there ahead of time, and if no one else can be found to acquire that position, the market maker can take the deal. For any single stock on the Nasdaq, there may be several market makers facing the same situation, because each particular stock may have several brokerages with the same intent. In other words, there comes a time when many brokerage accounts may have the same problem with a specific stock.

If a certain Nasdaq stock has three or four market makers, these market makers will know what the others are doing. There is no law against this, but it can be considered crooked since individual investors have no way of getting this type of information. However, by simply knowing what has been said here, an investor can take note of the close and apply some common sense.

Finally, let us consider the situation when the stock closes right at the high of the day. Those big trades at the close may represent buy orders from people that have shorted and are on margin calls. The market maker can easily sell that stock to the investor that has to cover the short position.

If the dealer wants, he can actually short the stock to anyone that has to buy. If investors are extremely bullish and feel that the stock will go even higher on the following day, they will buy on the close. This gives the market maker the incentive to take the market lower in the following session. You must keep in mind that the market maker already knows how much strength there is either above or below that closing price. Therefore, beware of a close at the high or low of the day, because it may lead to a reversal.

Cushing and Madhavan (2000), who happen to be well-known financial researchers, stated the following:

> On November 12, 1998, Safeway stock was to be added as of the close to the S&P 500, following an announcement made the previous week. High demand by index funds seeking to add Safeway stock to their portfolios at the closing price on this day resulted in a large order imbalance at the close. To accommodate the excess demand, the NYSE specialist for Safeway, Spear Leeds, set a closing price of $55, up 11% from the previous trade. In subsequent overnight trading Safeway stock fell in price, closing at $51.1875 the following day. Many institutional investors who paid large premiums to acquire Safeway at the close on November 11, were highly critical of the manner in which the closing price was determined.

This sort of activity becomes legal because the market maker can always show that there was some sort of imbalance. However, it was never revealed if whether or not the specialist shorted once the first public sale was executed. The point here should be plain enough since the specialist certainly did not maintain an orderly market at the close by allowing a jump of 11%. As can be seen, public funds are almost always going to be abused almost as much as individual investors. It was just another case, out of many hundreds, of being legally crooked.

21

SPECULATION

There is a difference between speculation and gambling although most people consider them to mean the same. However, while speculation involves a calculating, intellectual effort, gambling involves games of chance in which luck is the ruling factor. Of course, in both speculation and gambling, there are elements of both chance and reason. A major distinction is that in gambling, the amount of the bet is totally lost if one is wrong, which is not necessarily true in speculation.

In speculation, there is no infallible plan to make fortunes. There are no physical and mathematical formulas to follow. Since speculation is an art, it involves your inner self; your spirit; your mind. You must rely on yourself and follow your own convictions. You must not place all your trust on your brokerage firm, on your banker, on your newspaper, or on your government. You must assume all the responsibility for your money if you are going to be successful in speculation.

An essential quality of a speculator is courage. Courage is simply the confidence to act on a decision made by the reasoning powers of your mind. Courage in gambling is not the same as courage applied to speculation.

Having common sense or a good degree of good judgment is a requirement in speculation. Everything that is emotional or anxiety must not become part of the speculator for these things will interfere with good judgment. The ability to reason must exercise control over emotion.

You must also possess a fair degree of prudence which should be in balance with courage. It is generally agreed that prudence is the measuring of danger with alertness. A balance between risk and reward must be drawn.

Finally, flexibility is required which is simply the ability to change an opinion or a position. It is the power to reject ego, to admit a mistake as quickly as possible. Once a mistake has been realized, you should quit.

Since all of these qualities are of equal importance, they must be balanced within the speculator. A deficiency in any one of them will heavily increase the probability of defeat. Of course, not many people possess all of these qualities in proper balance. It is for this reason that few people succeed while many may fail. This can apply to stock speculation, business venturing or to personal matters.

There are several general laws in speculation which should be followed. These are to be considered universal laws. Follow these rules.

First of all, when in doubt, either reduce your position or do not invest. If your mind is not completely positive, there may be a good reason for it. The amount of your position may be too great for your means. There may also be factors which simply go against the grain of your market theory.

The important thing is to listen to your subconscious mind (sixth sense) which has nothing to do with emotion but deals with mental sensitivity instead. It does require a sixth sense in order to keep in tune with the elements of deceit.

You should not overtrade with very limited resources. Since continual mental control is necessary, you must not allow your judgment to be ruled by the fear of losing your entire savings.

It is not smart to average down unless there is strong evidence of accumulation. In other words, you should not continue to buy more of something if it continues to decline. To "buy down" in this fashion is to follow a downtrend. You must be capable of admitting that a downtrend has been established, and then you must discipline yourself to save as much as possible of the initial investment.

If you are going to be a true speculator, you must learn how to accept a loss. Prices do gyrate. If your reasoning was good from the start, the price will always come back. If your reasoning has been proven wrong, then you must learn to accept it and resign from the position. You must ask yourself if whether or not you would buy that same issue in the present at the current price, or would you rather acquire something else with better prospects.

When you do take a loss, there is a tendency to get right back into the market in order to make up the loss. Quite often, this is the worst thing to do resulting in still another loss. When a loss is incurred and the position is sold, you must stand back and do nothing until your mind is clear again. The anxiety of waiting may be painful but it is part of the discipline. It is much more painful to take another loss which can lead to demoralization.

It may not be very smart to invest in an industry once the public has recognized it to be a "hot market." Once the public recognizes a good thing, the situation is no longer to be considered "easy money." Therefore, you must learn not to follow the public.

It is not advised to trade in more stocks than can be properly watched and observed on the trading tape. Even if you choose up to ten favorites, it must certainly be reasonable to assume that only a few of those are truly in perfect situations that will maximize your investment.

Even if all the stocks on your list have been under heavy accumulation, you must still choose those two or three issues that have the best chance to double or triple your money. The ideal price range of those stocks would be between ten and thirty dollars per share. The problem with low price stocks is that they may take longer to advance, but the advantage is that once they do move, it becomes easier to double your money. The problem with high price issues is that it may take much longer to double your money if you hold, but the advantage is that these issues may be more volatile to the upside. The most ideal situation is a low-price issue that has at one time in the not too distant past been much higher in price. This

111

indicates that there is at least a capability of going much higher. The ideal price support of such a stock would be at a price range of say 12 to 17.

Since speculation is an art, the speculative game cannot be won consistently by mathematical formulation. It is not smart to place all your confidence in figures or statistics, for they can be deceiving. The numbers which are the most relevant are never clearly defined to the public. For example, attempting to formulate big block trades on an uptick versus a downtick is almost completely useless, because the New York Stock Exchange does not reveal to the public whether the big block was a purchase, sale or short-sale by the specialist. A big block purchase by the specialist on an uptick is bullish, but a big block short-sale on an uptick is bearish. Furthermore, a specialist short-sale will most likely occur when the stock is up for the day, but many traditional analysts believe that big blocks to the upside are always bullish. However, it does make a big difference whether or not the specialist is buying or selling. If the mathematical genius does not know the true circumstances of the trade, the numbers become totally useless. There are many technical indicators which do not take into account the activity of the stock specialist.

The important factor is to know well how your stocks operate. It is a good strategy to vary your investment between those few issues that interest you. The number of issues should be enough so that if some go out of favor you will always have others to consider without having to jump into some other unknown situation.

If an advance occurs in the market, there is a good chance that at least one of your favorites will advance. You can then add support to those issues that react the most favorable.

Simply stay with those issues that you know well. If ever you should find yourself buying out of anxiety or greed to make money, you should withdraw from the market and rest. Quite often, a speculator may go through a lucky streak which often leads to a period of carelessness. Even if you make a lot of money with the spirit described in this book, you must never get carried away and begin to invest simply for the sake of being in the market. Doing so is to invite disaster. Do not increase risk with an increase in profits. It is wrong to ever believe that you are able to afford more risk.

Are there stocks that you should watch even if you have no intention of buying them? Of course, there are. You should keep a chart of each individual Dow stock in order to determine what each specialist is doing. Although the Dow average is important, the individual issues of the Dow are even more important to observe.

If the Dow is going to new highs with only the help of a few issues, the odds favor that the advance will fail. There are times when the rally will look strong, but this too can be just an illusion. Of course, some of the Dow issues can be so oversold that a mere two or three-point advance in each of those can amplify the Dow tremendously and cause the Dow to advance through a major resistance level.

Of course, this same situation does have a long-term meaning which may be opposite to the short-term effect. Eventually, the oversold issues will become so great that a bottom will occur in the Dow and a major advance will begin. At this point, there may be only a few stocks near the highs with a few more at supports just below the high and the rest at support levels near the yearly lows. A rally in the low issues to prior highs would create a major advance of incredible proportions.

Keep in mind that the Dow average has become highly inflated. This situation has occurred because of the many stock splits in the Dow issues. With each split that occurs, volatility increases. Also, certain Dow stocks have been replaced by more volatile issues. This inflated situation helps the cause for those that operate the legally crooked system. It means that the averages can be amplified tremendously with mere fractional movements of each member stock within the Dow Jones Industrials or S&P 500. In other words, what may seem like a very big rally in the average may only represent minor advances in key stock issues. Therefore, the investor should notice the relationship of these factors whenever there is a volatile advance or decline in the major averages.

22

CONTRARIANISM

There is a belief that history repeats itself, and there certainly is abundant evidence that people so often make the same mistakes over and over again. It is unfortunate that in the stock market people so often do not learn by their experiences nor from history. Why is it that in the market more so than in any other field of endeavor, people do not learn to improve their performance? Certainly, a good portion of the answer must be related to the elements of greed, fear, and anxiety. In essence, the ability to properly judge the market is constantly being impaired by emotion. Furthermore, there are no set formulas, and there are no management textbooks. It is simply not like anything taught in high school or college.

The select few who operate from the inside have always been able to manipulate the great masses of people by exploiting their greatest weakness which is the madness that is inherent in crowds. The madness of crowds is, of course, derived from man's inability to control emotion. It is also peculiar that the practicing of weakness or emotion in financial matters is in itself a source of psychological security. Although the crowd exercises the weaknesses of greed, fear, and anxiety, the crowd does represent a feeling of security to each individual of the crowd. In other words, an individual experiences fear in making a decision alone. However, when many people make a decision to act, then the observer senses a feeling of anxiety to join the group.

When the market is at the bottom, the individual is not inclined to buy, because not many other people are buying at that time. It is human nature. It feels better to buy when everyone else is buying, usually near the top of the market. It can rightfully be said that people in a crowd are much like sheep and that SHEEP FEEL BETTER BEING SLAUGHTERED AS A GROUP. In essence, this is the great pitfall of each individual who joins that great institution called "the buying public."

Stock market diagnosis is not complete without considering the contrarian view along with market psychology. When almost every adviser sees something the same way, it is the contrarian concept to consider doing the opposite, or perhaps in some cases to do nothing at all. It may be more appropriate to say that one should simply not do what everyone else is doing.

Greed and fear are the two most important tools used by manipulators. Actually, this attribute of greed and fear is used as a weapon against the public through the use of appropriate market action and the news media. An understanding of greed and fear should be a basic requirement in any study of the financial world. It is unfortunate that such a study is not considered important enough by educators to be included in school textbooks.

People quite often buy out of greed, and they sell when in fear. Knowing this, the manipulator or the opposing force can now exploit these weaknesses that are inherent in the masses. It is part of human nature to buy when everything looks promising and to sell when everything looks worse. Whenever you entertain the idea of buying, ask yourself the following question: Does it feel obvious that the market is going up? If the answer is yes, do not enter the market.

At this point, it is important to understand the element of risk and how it relates to greed and fear. First of all, whatever is psychological may be the opposite of what is a reality. For example, as greed increases in one's mind, the risk is perceived as having decreased. In reality, risk has actually increased with greed. As basic as all this may sound, people will simply not practice these basic mental concepts at critical market junctures.

The combination of greed and fear is the most commonly used weapon on earth. Many battles have been lost by physically stronger armies on account of greed and fear. Since the public is fragmented and lacks union, it can be steered by radio, TV, and newspapers. Of course, we should not dismiss the significance of rumor. Whatever the case may be, it is the news media that initiates and controls greed and fear. To figure out who actually is responsible, one need only look to see who owns and operates the media firms and who is affiliated with these operations.

Let us look closer to see how greed and fear operate within the market. The general pattern is most always the same. However, it is always obscured by the emotion of investors. There is always excessive greed at the top of the market and excessive fear at the bottom. This cycle goes on and on through time.

During the first half of a bull market, the public exercises fear. Then the public exercises greed in the last stage of the bull market and maintains that greed into the first stage of a bear market. However, in the final stage of a bear market, the public succumbs to fear and exits the market. Fear then extends itself well into the early stages of a bull market.

There are short periods of time when even public sentiment might be profitable. Once the cake is eaten by the smart people, someone is needed to get rid of the scraps. This occurs in the last stage of the bull market. As stock prices reach for the top, many people do make profits if they sell at the top. However, most of those profits erode as the bear market takes effect.

Anxiety is an element that takes control of greed and fear from you. It steals your control by causing you to make a premature decision. Anxiety, also known as impatience, is one of the biggest problems of the average trader. The best way to combat anxiety is to form an objective of your entering point and practice discipline.

You must discipline yourself to become more and more fearful as prices go higher and higher. When you are waiting to buy, you must learn to feel better and better as prices go lower. Market extremes are opportunities.

You must learn to control emotion. You must be prepared to do the opposite of the general mood, provided you are aware of the market stages and cycles. Do not feel that you must be in the market at all times. Get out of the market at times to regain your perspective and unprejudiced view of the situation. Emotion will blind you when making a decision.

When prices are highest and sentiment is most bullish, the public wants bullish news, and it gets bullish news. If you absorb this news, get enthusiastic and buy to make some easy money, you are surrendering to the element of greed. The same thing occurs, but only in reverse, when bearish news amplifies the element of fear.

Many people do not wish to believe that the smart money group represents a conspiracy since this would imply that a crime is being committed. However, since this type of conspiracy is in the gray area of the law, most people prefer to think of it as being part of the game. Whatever your opinion, you must believe that there are varied groups in the market that do take advantage of events and conditions through the use of greed and fear. The important thing for you to know is simply to recognize when the market is appealing to the sense of greed or the sense of fear.

In the scientific sense, the top of a market, where bullish sentiment is the highest, can be explained as that point where sellers become more numerous than buyers. At the same time, the sentiment is very high which means that most people are apt to be buyers. The problem is that most people have already bought into the market and are merely holding. Thus, the illusion of strength continues. At this point, the market becomes vulnerable to any outside force. The control establishment or any other powerful syndicate, depending on whether it is stock related or real estate related, can easily unload into whatever demand is left and fully drain that demand. Can this be accomplished by conspiracy, or is it simply a natural occurrence? It can most certainly be simply a natural occurrence. It can also be accomplished by the intervention of a powerful and well-capitalized force. If the intervention is by conspiracy, is it legal? The buyer must always beware when entering an open market. However, the buyer cannot be aware of anything if the perpetration of a devious act is either partially or completely hidden. It simply becomes another case of being legally crooked.

Advisory Sentiment

An advisory analyst is usually a private service that offers either a written or online newsletter for a fee. This category is mentioned here, not because these individuals are in any way tied to the control establishment, but because their actions are related directly or indirectly to the actions of brokerage establishments.

The consensus of advisory services is considered a form of analysis and should be part of every stock market diagnosis. The overall sentiment of analysts and newsletter writers is actually used as a contrary indicator. There is a correlation between sentiment and market movement. Sentiment is highest at market tops because most advisors find security in being trend followers.

When forming a diagnosis, you can look at the number of advisors that are bullish or bearish. In general, if the number of bulls is below 60 percent, you can be reasonably assured that the market has not reached a long-term top. However, whenever the percentage of bulls reaches the 60 percent level, it is cause for an alert over the near term. If the bulls reach within the 60 to 70 percent level, it will represent a bearish warning, especially if the bears drop to under 20 percent. When looking for a bear market low, a figure approaching 40 percent of bears may be considered a bullish alert. Of course, care must be taken depending on the survey service being used for the advisories. Investors Intelligence, founded by Abe Cohen in 1963, is a primary source for data of this nature.

Of course, this sentiment indicator must never be used entirely on its own. It must be used in conjunction with the other material contained in this book. Your diagnosis can only be justified when your conclusion is confirmed by all of your methods involving market maker analysis, block volume reversal, charting, technical formulations and sentiment indicators. Consider the following quote by John Maynard Keynes. "The market can stay irrational longer than you can stay solvent." This means that any contrarian belief must be accompanied by either a long process of accumulation or distribution, or it must relate to indicators that will actually show signs of either weakness or underlying strength. Amidst all of this, keep in mind that not all stocks will top or bottom at the same time.

When a contrary opinion is formed, the investor must remember that it does take time for a long-term trend to turn, or reverse (Neill, 2001). In other words, the public is not wrong during a trend which can last for some time. Of course, extremely heavy volume, well above the average, will be one of the best indicators to place yourself on alert.

Humphrey Neill, in his book, "The Art of Contrary Thinking," says, "Obvious thinking, or thinking the same way in which everyone else is thinking, commonly leads to wrong judgments and wrong conclusions." He goes on to say that you should learn to think contrarily. Emphasis should be placed on the idea of learning to think contrarily, and not accept contrary thinking as a blanket statement.

There have been many famous people who have fostered contrarian beliefs. Sir John Templeton, who passed away on July 8, 2008, at the age of 95, was famous for his investment strategies that ran counter to the general consensus. One of his best quotes that can be found at several Internet sources goes as follows, "Bull markets are born in pessimism, grow on skepticism, mature on optimism, and die of euphoria." Another quote by Templeton goes, "To buy when others are despondently selling and sell when others are greedily buying requires the greatest fortitude and pays the greatest reward." Those two quotes alone represent the heart of contrarianism.

Considering the nature of contrary thinking and the apparent validity of its importance, one should be able to envision the obvious conclusion. Public sentiment can most certainly be used as a weapon by the brokerage establishment against the investor. As a result, this type of situation can easily be classified as being legally crooked.

23

RULES AND REGULATIONS

According to the NYSE, its board-of-directors selects specialists on the basis of their ability to maintain an orderly market and on their capital resources. Many people in our population could easily be qualified according to these standards. Of course, the NYSE says nothing concerning its policy of expressing favoritism. As far as capital is concerned, the rules have stated that specialists must have enough capital to buy a five thousand share position in each stock which they maintain. Needless to say, a five thousand share position is small compared to specialist activity.

Before the turn of the century, the selection of a specialist was really quite irrelevant since most of them were established as firms at the NYSE a long time ago. Once established as a specialist firm, it continued under the control of the families involved (from father to son). The stock specialist system was comparable to a royal succession which had little or nothing to do with a democratic form of politics. To get expelled, a specialist firm had to be so careless as to endanger the power position of the others or compromise the operation of the NYSE.

Things changed rather rapidly once the big investment banking firms began to realize the potential for gain. The NYSE chose not to restrict the ownership of specialist firms, because it sensed that the big banking firms would bring in more money into the system. The buying of the individual specialist partnerships caused a series of mergers until only seven major firms remained. Of course, the individual principals of each specialist firm did get very wealthy as a result of each sale, and the employees now had even more incentive to generate much more revenue than ever before. In essence, this became the problem that would eventually ruin the whole system.

The people that operated the old specialist system were expert in the art of the illusion. They were people that specifically knew how to operate expertly in covert operations while bending key rules and regulations of the NYSE. The specialist system was an art form to be admired. It represented the ultimate smoothness in the process of being legally crooked.

FleetBoston Bank, which merged into Bank of America, formed a specialist group, along with Bear Stearns, until finally, Goldman Sachs bought into the system. While the NYSE hailed the entrance of these super powers, it failed to realize that power leads to abuse. These people that were taking over the specialist system were hacks, compared to the old partnerships, in every sense of the word. These new entrants were hacks because they allowed making money to rule their lives while sacrificing the art of illusion. It became a matter of who made the most revenue for the sake of being promoted up the chain of the parent company. The abuse was no longer artistically hidden as in the past. It was allowed to proceed over the border of criminality.

Members of the New York Stock Exchange are regulated by the NYSE board-of-directors. The system operates by self-regulation while complying with the overall principles of the Securities and Exchange Commission. According to the NYSE, stock specialists are subject to many rules. The following represents some of the rules.

1. A specialist cannot buy or sell for his own account at the same price as a customer's limit order.
2. A specialist cannot buy or sell for his own account if holding unexecuted market orders for customers.
3. A specialist cannot directly accept orders in stocks in which he specializes, from the principal stockholders, directors or officers of the corporation. This rule also applies to pension funds, banks or investment firms.

It must be kept in mind that even the most stringent regulations can often be circumvented by the interpretation (loopholes) of the local authority and confirmed by the inaction of the higher authority. One must never believe that a set of laws is a guarantee of public good.

A specialist is allowed to buy big blocks after the closing of the market without the trade appearing on the tape. If a trader wants to sell a large block, his broker will contact the specialist. If the specialist is willing to buy it, he will most likely bid below the market (for example, one-half point below). This trade will take place after the close and is reported in the weekly volume for the specialist. The trade will not appear on the tape.

While the seller feels rid of a problem, the specialist has a built-in profit. The specialist can easily sell the stock by breaking the big block into a series of small blocks. This can all be done by the following morning so that financing the shares is not a problem. Depending on the size of the block and of a rally, the profit can be quite stupendous. This can all be done so quickly that he may not even have to finance the stock that was bought. Not many people have this type of advantage in trading stock.

A specialist firm is paid commission on all trades. It receives a cut of the amount from the commission house. This is one reason why the smaller specialist firms did so well. These people were more than satisfied with their profits since they kept the money for themselves. The larger firms that took over were not satisfied with these same profits, because much more revenue was needed to pay for their investment into the NYSE.

The specialist must maintain a record of all buy and sell orders (the book) which is to be confirmed by the exchange twice a year. Each page was scaled in eighths with one full point covered, and of course, this changed with the introduction of decimal cents. For example, 50 would beat the top with 50 7/8 at the bottom. Orders to buy were on the left side with orders to sell on the right. Orders had to be listed in the order received with the name of the brokerage firm next to the proper price level.

NYSE Rule 92 does forbid specialists from entering proprietary orders when there are unexecuted customer orders at the same price. The two most common cases of abuse involving the actual breaking of the law can be identified as "trading ahead" and interpositioning." The act of "interpositioning" is illegal. This is a situation where a specialist or broker-dealer places him or herself between a buyer and seller to make a profit off their trade. "Trading ahead" is a situation where the specialist exercises discretion when he notices orders to buy or sell coming into the system from the floor and acts to either buy or short before those orders from the floor officially hit his system. These are the acts which caused charges to be brought against the specialists.

According to the rules, the orders in the book had to be confirmed by the exchange twice a year. However, overall inspections by exchange authorities were rare. Since the members of the floor were self-regulated, it is easy to see that specialists were not under constant scrutiny. All was fine so long as there were no complaints from outside parties. Whether or not a rule had been broken really became a matter of interpretation.

It is also important to note that most of the authority figures of the NYSE and SEC are people that have been tied to the securities industry. In other words, these are people who have worked for the major brokerage houses. This being true and easily verified as being true, anyone of common sense should easily be able to figure how the system really works. These people know each other well because they have associated with each other over the years.

Due Diligence

Every investor should know what is meant by due diligence. This issue is legally crooked because it tends to work in favor of the seller in the legal sense although it is meant to work in favor of the buyer in the eyes of the seller. Be careful with this issue, and take care to comprehend the real meaning of this law.

Although the definition can be written in various forms, the important thing is to realize that this law pertains to both seller and buyer. Most legal definitions may be similar to the following language. Due diligence is a time measurement of activity devoted to prudence, as properly to be expected from, and ordinarily exercised by, a reasonable person under the particular circumstances; not measured by any absolute standard but depends on the relative facts of the case. In other words, to the buyer, due diligence means "making sure that you are getting what you believe you are paying for." To the seller, it means that the selling party must provide relevant answers to any questions posed by the buyer. Therefore, the seller must continually be ready to prove the absence of any problems. If there are any problems or negatives, the seller must divulge those issues on written statements known as disclosures.

The issue of due diligence has two sides. Therefore, the seller must exercise due diligence by determining if the buyer is really qualified in buying the product. Furthermore, the seller must disclose all of the facts about the product. Then, in reverse of this, the seller must determine if the investment is as good as what is being portrayed in the offering.

These rules will be initiated whenever a new stock offering is being presented to the public by an investment banker. The investment banker or brokerage firm does not wish to be sued by disgruntled investors if a material fact is not disclosed. The period of due diligence which could cover several weeks works to the advantage of the seller because it gives the buyer enough time to consider the offering. The problem is that many investors do not spend the necessary time to do a good job of either asking questions or thoroughly investigating the offering. The investor should never come to believe that he is at fault simply because he had been given a certain amount of time to investigate the offering. If a material fact is ever not divulged to the investor in writing, it means that the investor may have a case against the seller.

Brokerage firm agents are thoroughly indoctrinated on the importance of maintaining legality. The broker securities examination devotes a whole section to the law. The purpose of this training is not so much to protect the investor as it is to protect the brokerage firm as the seller or provider of the service.

24

TECHNICAL ANALYSIS

Charting goes hand-in-hand with market maker analysis or block-volume reversal analysis. A chart will reveal in vivid form the path which has been taken by the smart money element. On a chart, you can easily see the volume and the price level and can determine support and resistance levels along with significant patterns.

Market makers do make use of technical analysis and charting. Stock specialists will quite often make use of support levels to accumulate. The lower end of a support level offers them the best opportunities because the biggest sell stops are usually located at the lower range and perhaps just below a recognized support level.

A chart will most always help the speculator to anticipate the market maker establishment. However, the chartist, who believes in market maker analysis, must separate himself from the crowd of traditional technical analysts once the chart is drawn and is ready for final judgment. Because technical analysis has such a wide following, it could be used as a weapon by the specialist or other manipulators to trap technical analysts into making the wrong decision.

The manipulating operator can easily strive to create false buy and sell signals. In this respect, the method of specialist analysis involves artistic ability and a feel for the game. The one who practices this philosophy must be able to adjust to the many variables that will come into contention.

The three analysis techniques are fundamental, technical, and sentiment. While some writers may stress that these are all separate issues, it should be kept in mind that there is relativity between the three methods. It is true that each technique is carried out free of the others. However, to form a full picture of the maze, one should relate the situation of one with the other. For example, if technical analysis is showing an upward move to an old high on very heavy volume with every analyst on a buy recommendation as a quarterly report is about to be issued, then this should be cause for concern. It becomes a case where all three methods of analysis come into play and become related to a forthcoming event. This relativity is what becomes the essence of the study of stock market illusionology.

Technical analysis and a little common sense will always help you to make the close calls. For example, let us consider the following situation. A stock which has been in a bullish trend experiences a correction. Then you observe that the price reverses upward after a day or two of heavy big block activity at the lows. Meanwhile, you feel that it should go to new highs because of a bullish configuration on the chart and because the volume was light when at recent highs. However, after a short rally, you begin to see big blocks crossing the tape on a steadily increasing price. What do you do? Is the specialist gearing for a decline so soon? No, not necessarily. It could be straight selling from his inventory, or it could even represent further accumulation.

If you believe that the objective of the specialist is for a much higher price level, then you can reason that he wants to pull the stock back (not back to the lows) a little in order to replenish his inventory. You should not consider it a block-volume reversal when you see big blocks crossing the tape in an incoherent manner. Since every situation will be different, you should simply be on alert whenever you witness big blocks and heavy volume, and then try to relate to the probable objective of the specialist. Examples of charting can be found in the addendum section of this book.

Stochastics Oscillator

The Stochastic Oscillator was developed by George Lane in the late 1950s. It is a momentum indicator that shows the location of the close relative to the high-low range over a set number of time periods. According to Lane, the Stochastic Oscillator does not follow price, and it does not follow volume. Instead, it follows the speed or the momentum of price. As a rule, the momentum changes direction before price. This means that bullish and bearish divergences in the Stochastic Oscillator can be used to predict reversals. The Stochastic Oscillator is range bound which makes it useful for identifying overbought and oversold levels, especially if very heavy volume occurs at the high or low on the oscillator.

Divergences on the Stochastics Oscillator occur when a new high or low in the price of the issue is not confirmed by the Stochastic Oscillator. A bullish divergence occurs when price shows a lower low, but the Stochastic Oscillator forms a higher low. This shows less downside momentum that could be predicting a bullish reversal. A bearish divergence forms when price shows a higher high, but the Stochastic Oscillator forms a lower high. This shows less upside momentum that could predict a bearish reversal. Once a divergence takes hold, you should look for a confirmation to signal an actual reversal. A bearish divergence can be confirmed with a support break on the price chart or a Stochastic Oscillator break below 50, which is the centerline. A bullish divergence can be confirmed with a resistance break on the price chart or a stochastic oscillator break above 50.

The middle area of 50 is an important level to watch. The Stochastic Oscillator moves between zero and one hundred, which makes 50 the centerline. A cross above 50 signals that prices are trading in the upper half of their high-low range for the given period. This implies that the cup is half full. Conversely, a cross below 50 means price is trading in the bottom half of the given period. This implies that the cup is half empty. In conclusion, this indicator is a requirement for any trader so long as the trader is willing to relate this issue with other facets of analysis.

Moving Average Convergence/Divergence (MACD)

The MACD was developed by Gerald Appel. This indicator should be used as part of the discipline in evaluating exchange insider intentions. The MACD is composed of two lines on a chart although three lines are used to calculate the result. The fast line, which is called the MACD line, is the difference between two exponentially smoothed moving averages of closing prices. The slow line, which is called the signal line, is a smoothed average of the MACD line.

When the fast line crosses over the slow line, it becomes a buy signal. When the fast line crosses below the slow line, it is a sell signal. The MACD also acts as an oscillator with a central zero point. It may indicate overbought or oversold conditions. When the reading is below the zero level, a bullish crossover may indicate the optimal point to buy. This indicator should be used along with stochastics to determine if there is a correlation of signals.

Specialist Indicators

Mathematics and statistics can be used to supplement specialist analysis. In this respect, Barron's can be of practical use for its presentation of market statistics, especially those concerning specialist and public short sales. Since the exchanges lag in time before releasing data on specialist activity, the numbers are not as valuable as they would be if current. However, the figures have proven to be of great help, and the indicators derived from those figures have proven to be valid. The indicators are in the form of ratios; however, readers of this work are invited to formulate their own indicators. A major problem is that the Nasdaq market makers operate in secret with not much data being released on their positions. It is for this reason that the deceit and corruption will continue to flourish throughout the Nasdaq market which has become more dynamic than the NYSE.

The following section is for learning purposes only since it comes from old data. However, this data does prove the connection that NYSE specialists enjoyed by using all of their privileges. It is up to the reader to simply understand that this is what occurred, or it is up to the reader formulate his or her own methods into the future while adjusting for changes that may occur at the trading level.

THE SPECIALIST SHORT SALES RATIO

The specialist short sales ratio is the number produced by dividing specialist short sales by total short sales (SS/TS). Usually, these readings will range from 40 to 50 percent. In a bull market, the reading will average closer to the 40 percent level. A lower number represents bullishness. Whenever the reading drops below 40 percent, it is indicating that the probability is very high for a market advance in the near future. Some researchers have found that any reading below 35 percent represents close to a 100 percent probability of a market advance over the following three to six months.

Although the values will oscillate from week to week, the mere reaching of a low reading is enough to place an investor on alert. Of course, the weekly readings can be averaged over ten or twenty weeks to form a trend, or they can be plotted individually on a graph. A low reading over a period of three or four weeks is definitely a bullish signal that must not be ignored.

Let us consider some examples from the bull market during 1986.

SEP 5   40.1%
    12   39.2% Accumulation begins on public selling
    19   39.0%
    26   35.0% Alert that market will hold
OCT 3   34.7% Public short sales heavy at the lows
    10   34.7% Confirming that market will hold
    17   41.3%
    24   37.1% Public short sales were heavy
    31   41.0%
NOV 7   35.8% Public short sales very heavy
    14   30.5% Dow at 1800 level
    21   35.1% Specialist accumulation at the lows
    28   44.6%
DEC 5   44.4%
    12   40.6%
    19   46.2% Specialist accumulation at the lows of the market
    26   38.4% Alerting for an advance
JAN 2   30.6% Starting major advance from 1900 level

When the market is going to be bearish for several months, the readings simply do not dip below 40 percent on a steady basis. Furthermore, the unweighted average will trend steadily to higher levels.

This period in time represented an accumulation period in which specialists and other smart money people were buying as public investors and fund managers were selling. The overall mood was geared to be negative which is usual when the public sells and exchange insiders buy.

All of this indicated that specialists were looking for a major advance over the following year. In six months, the Dow rose 500 points.

Over the years, heavier volume figures have affected the range of readings just a little. In a bull market, a reading of 45% can still be considered to be very bullish. However, a reading above 50% should represent an alert and anything approaching 60% should be cause for worry.

Let us now observe how the numbers match together with the increased volume figures of the year 1998.

	Spec. Shorts	Total Shorts	% Reading
OCT 23	220,378,000	413,787,000	53.3%
30	192,512,000	393,428,000	48.9%
NOV 6	236,619,000	470,776,000	50.3%
13	162,069,000	347,688,000	46.6%
20	189,829,000	397,172,000	47.8%
27	136,312,000	271,827,000	50.1%
DEC 4	165,661,000	369,598,000	44.8%
11	145,987,000	324,218,000	45.0%
18	165,177,000	362,447,000	45.6%

OTHER POSSIBLE RATIOS

The short sales ratios work better in calling bullish signals. In other words, bullish readings are more significant than bearish ones. However, you would want to see the regular continuation of bullish numbers in a bull market. In a bear market, you would be looking for a strong bullish reading which could signify a bullish reversal. Any of these ratios which compare the short sales activity work well at major lows.

As a supplement to these ratios, a public to specialist short sales ratio can also be used (PS/SS). In this case, a high number would represent bullishness. Since specialists will most always short sell in greater volume as compared to the public, the reading should stay well below 100 percent. The reader should, of course, keep in mind that adjustments will always have to be made over a period of time to allow for activity changes in the market.

A range between 40 to 70 percent is a normal reading in a bull market. A reading of over 80 percent is to be considered extremely bullish. Such a high reading is rare, but it does occur about once or twice per year during a bull market. For example, on the week of January 2, 1987, which was the start of a major advance, public short sales were 9,781,500 shares, and specialist short sales were 10,544,800 shares, which gave a reading of 92.8%. It becomes easy to see that the public has no business shorting as much as specialists. The investor should keep in mind that specialists will short for very small periods while the public will be shorting for longer periods. In other words, a specialist may cover a short position with a very minor decline.

Here is an even better example. For the week of October 25, 1985, the reading was 101.9 percent, which meant that public short sales were greater than those of the specialist. This situation is truly rare. Such a reading should have given faith even to the extremely fainthearted. When this occurred, the Dow was at the 1360 level where it had lingered for some time. The mood was negative, and there was much talk of a big decline. However, the short sales indicator proved to be true, because by December 31, the Dow had advanced by 200 points which represented a major advance in those days.

THE SHORT SALES OSCILLATOR

An oscillator-type of chart is produced by using at least two of the short sales ratios. I prefer to use the specialist short sales and the public short sales ratios. Since the physical conditions of the market do change over time, this material is being entered here for historical purposes only. It becomes evident that specialists did know what they were doing in preparation for future events. The formulation is presented below.

READING = PUBLIC SHORTS / MEMBER SHORTS - SPECIALIST SHORTS / TOTAL SHORTS

Once the public ratio is subtracted from the specialist ratio, the resulting number can be plotted on a chart. Of course, if one does not enjoy the making of charts, a simple table can be constructed. The following is from the year 1985 and shown here for historical evidence.

	PS	MS	PS/MS	SS	TS	SS/TS	
OCT 25	15,450,000	32,358,600 .	477	15,164,900	47,808,600	.317	+.160
NOV 1	11,483,000	34,952,100 .	303	19,136,800	49,435,100	.387	-.084
NOV 8	10,943,800	45,523,700 .	257	20,798,200	53,467,500	.389	-.132
NOV 15	15,811,800	55,903,300 .	283	28,267,100	71,715,100	.396	-.113
NOV 22	21,244,200	46,393,100	.458	22,753,200	67,637,300	.336	+.122
NOV 29	10,077,600	28,503,900 .	458	13,003,500	38,581,500	.337	+.121

The reading for October 25, 1985, was one of the strongest readings ever produced by this indicator. It was one of those rare situations when both ratios united together in a very bullish fashion. Despite all of the negativism in the news, this indicator was showing a building of strength behind the scenes.

You can see that the reading for November 22, and 29, confirmed the bullish situation. You can also see that the public was short selling heavily. This bullish set of conditions was just one of many such indications produced by my short sales oscillator.

Placing classifications on certain numerical levels can be a matter of opinion, and they would always be subject to change according to the times. Taking the changes in the market into account, the following is just a suggestion. Throughout the future, adjustments can be made to the final analysis according to the new trading patterns of the future.

Extremely Bullish............. +.300
Very Bullish.................... +.200
Bullish.......................... +.100
Trend Alert..................... +.000
Trend Alert..................... -.100
Bearish Alert.................... -.200
Bearish.......................... -.250
Very Bearish.................... -.300

Throughout the early bull market starting in 1982, my short sales oscillator was able to forecast every major advance.

Although this indicator is useful on a continual basis, it becomes most valuable in determining the approach of a bear market low. It continues to be of value through the middle stages of a bull market in determining further advances. It even becomes valuable in the last stages of a bull market when the readings fail to show strength on the advances.

It does require the art of interpretation to maximize this indicator. It is much like a polygraph. The movements of the readings should be matched with other occurrences within and/or outside the market. The reader must also, according to the times, determine the amount of lag time between the time of the reading and the market's probable reaction.

The technical indicators presented here are valid because they involve the short sale which is the most important tool of those in control. Furthermore, the short sale is the most relevant factor in the market mix, because it forms a direct relationship between the public and exchange insiders. The relationship is that the smart money will strive to bottom the market at that point where the public has been short selling the most in comparison to exchange members. It is a very relevant contra-association in which the odds are in favor of the market maker who knows the location of the short sales. In conclusion, the short sale is the greatest tool of the specialist or any market maker.

DOW ANALYSIS

It is highly advisable that readers place importance on observing the individual components of the Dow. An investor who considers himself serious about the market should maintain charts on all thirty Dow stocks. It becomes important to know in what manner the Dow is being driven either up or down in order to determine the strength of the momentum. Of course, it is up to the reader to apply some common sense in making this analysis. It is really very easy to do and does not require much in the way of professional experience.

When an advance is occurring, count the issues that are going to new highs along with those coming off oversold conditions. The advance could be an illusion of strength carried out by many weaklings that may be just bouncing off very oversold conditions. If those weaklings are many, those stocks alone could donate many points toward an advance that is doomed to fail. This will be true if the market is simply not going through accumulation.

An advance may be much more credible when the majority of Dow stocks are pushing through mid-ranges in their price patterns. This would indicate that many more Dow issues may be driven to new highs or to prior highs. At least it would indicate a better chance of breaking through meaningful resistance levels with more participation of the components.

Of course, it will always be important to inspect each Dow component for accumulation or distribution. It is truly amazing that so many Dow components do not follow the pattern of the Dow average. However, it only takes a few Dow components to affect the Dow average greatly.

25

ECONOMIC INDICATORS

This topic could easily cover a whole book. However, since the purpose of this book is simply to alert the investment community, only the basics of the major economic reports and indicators will be researched. The most important issue presented here is for the reader to understand with the conviction that so many of the economic reports initiated by the government are legally crooked. Whether this problem originated by deceitful design or by innocent practice, the fact remains that numbers within a statistical platform can be deceiving which falls within the definition of crooked. On the other side of the same coin, it is also a fact that because the numbers follow a designated formula, the results, however deceiving, fall within the definition of being legal. All of this leads to the greatest problem of all which is that most of the public do not know the government's formulation and are not made aware of the dynamics of the reporting results.

Unemployment Rate

Released by the Bureau of Labor Statistics under the Department of Labor, the unemployment rate is one of the most popular economic-related monthly reports. Despite the important implications of this report, it is the one that is most misunderstood by the public. Most people actually believe that the unemployment rate represents the exact number of people that do not have jobs.

Officially, the unemployment rate represents how many people do not have jobs and are actively looking for a job. This means that you are technically not unemployed if you have not looked for a job. If you decide to seek employment, then, you are officially considered unemployed. Once your unemployment benefits run out, and you do not continue to look for a job, you will be considered no longer unemployed. As can easily be seen from these statements of fact, which come directly from the BLS, there are definite problems with the system.

The Bureau of Labor Statistics conducts a monthly survey called the Current Population Survey (CPS) to produce key numbers in order to calculate those that are employed or unemployed. This process has been used since 1940, and only the survey questions have changed. The actual page from the Bureau of Labor Statistics is presented for your review in the Addendum as Exhibit 7. The process takes the form of a survey done by the Census Bureau. The major problem with this method is that it does not account for people that have stopped looking for employment and all those that have simply left the system.

Each survey involves about 60,000 households out of a total listing of about 110,000 people. Approximately 2,200 government employees work each month to interview households in each sample group. There is nothing wrong with the sample number. However, you should read the exact method and decide where the problems may arise as to the validity of the system.

The conclusion to this study is that the unemployment rate will always tend to be inaccurate and tend to be understated. However, in good economic times, the deviation should tend to be minimal while in bad economic times the deviation should tend to be much greater than acceptable. Investors should simply realize this problem and realize that the real unemployment rate is much greater than what is being reported. Furthermore, investors should realize that although the reported rate may show improvement at some point in time, the actual situation may not really be that of improvement since more and more people are not being accounted as being unemployed.

There is a further implication to this. It is when the economy does actually turn for the better. At such a time, it becomes possible that those who have been unemployed and not accounted for being unemployed may at that time begin to seek employment which may cause a temporary increase in unemployment. This type of event could very well mask the real improvement in the economy. It could also cause investors to sell stock at a time when they should be buying. If the Bureau of Labor Statistics should ever come under pressure for the system that is being used, it will most likely make changes for the purpose of making it look good, but the end result will most likely be no better. Instead of considering unemployment (the tails of a coin), it may be better to more accurately measure and report the employment rate (the heads of a coin).

Gross Domestic Product and Gross National Product

Both GDP and GNP are defined as goods and services produced. However, they use different criteria for coverage. GDP involves goods and services that are produced by labor and property located in the United States. On the other hand, GNP involves goods and services produced by labor and property supplied by U.S. residents, which means that it counts toward GNP so long as the labor and property are supplied by U.S. residents even if they may be located abroad. As a result, GDP becomes the dominant index since it involves only production from within the nation. It takes into account employment, productivity, industrial output, and investment in equipment and structures.

The Gross Domestic Product (GDP) is the most followed business indicator and represents a broad measure of economic activity within the nation. GDP is reported by the Bureau of Economic Analysis (BEA) of the Department of Commerce. The elements of the GDP are actually within the makeup of the GNP, which means that if the GDP is corrupted with false theory, then the result of the GNP will become even more corrupt. Both of these reports fall into the same category of deception and misconception.

This is not meant to be directed against the Department of Commerce, because the people that work these jobs are dedicated to doing the best possible job to report on the available data. The problem comes from the political power that can be exerted upon the Department of Commerce. It must be remembered that the head of the Department of Commerce is someone that is appointed by the President of the United

States. Investors must simply be aware that manipulation is to be expected to some degree.

Measuring an economy by its sales revenue without taking into account such matters as efficiencies, productivity, cash flow and wealth becomes like a highway to nowhere. The activities of people and businesses should not be directed toward credit borrowing and mass consumption (Small Business Authority, 2011). For the sake of producing revenue, a nation imports more than it exports which ultimately weakens a nation. This means that trade deficits go higher while the GDP goes higher. A more valid indicator would measure the production of items that create more wealth than we currently consume. In other words, the idea is to create things that create value instead of consuming things that create no value. Measuring the consumption of items that do not contribute to the benefit of the nation is totally equal to following a false prophet.

Investors should consider that inflation becomes a major problem with GDP. If certain politicians can keep inflation numbers down, then the GDP can be manipulated to look better. If inflation is understated, then the inflation-adjusted rate of GDP growth gets reported higher. This can happen since the Federal Reserve has the power to understate inflation by using only those items that can make the desired result. It becomes a matter of interlinking of objectives between factions associated with the government and directed by the highest office in the land. Of course, it is crooked. It represents deviant behavior. It is legal because the government ordains it as a legal process. However, in the end, it can only be rationalized as legally crooked behavior.

There is evidence that the DGP has been continually used for political purposes by both political parties. It just depends who is in the presidential office. According to a written report by Walter J. Williams (2004), he says that Lyndon Johnson kept sending the initial GNP estimates back to the Department of Commerce for correction until he finally got the number he desired. He goes further to report that a senior member of the Executive Branch met with a senior officer of a large computer company and requested that computer sales be inflated to increase the GNP number. Another major problem that can only be considered highly suspicious is whenever the GDP and GNP are revised on a monthly basis. These revisions can only mean that the original number should never have been issued in the first place, and it also implies that maybe pressure has been applied against the Department of Commerce to make the number better than the original entry. This is the equivalent of getting the results of a school test, and then being allowed to look at the errors, and then being allowed to change the questions to make the answers correct.

26

CRASHES

It is often said by traditionalists that no one prospers from market crashes and sharp declines. News commentators always seem to emphasize that even stock specialists and other market makers take a beating. This is always concurred by an NYSE spokesperson on TV interviews. Of course, it is interesting to note that proof of this is never given and never verified. Totally absurd is the idea that no one makes money in declines and bear markets. It is a fact that specialists and other market makers do a lot of short selling each day. Therefore, who else could possibly gain more from a major decline?

Whenever a sharp decline occurs, people usually believe that specialists are taken by surprise or that they have lost control. Neither of these two beliefs could be further from the truth.

Before every crash and major decline, there has been heavy volume and/or big block activity. The big blocks are simply short sales by specialists and others who know very well what is going to occur. In other words, stock specialists intend to profit by a decline in one way or another. It may be by heavy short sales, by accumulating at lower prices or by getting rid of the competition. It could be all these things.

When a crash begins early in the trading session, stock specialists and other market makers do not support the market until near the close, or most likely, they wait until the open of the following session. Once market makers begin to buy at the lows, the market begins to hold and then advances. Since this advance is usually quite substantial, it can be concluded that market makers and close associates do make money on the situation.

Once a market maker has an inventory of short sales, he will not support the price upon seeing an increase in selling pressure from institutional concerns.

After a crash, as was the case in 1987, it is released through the news media that specialists are low on capital and are in need of financing. This is deceiving because it implies that they are broke. In reality, they may be low on capital, because they committed all of their funds at the bottom.

When a crash is in progress, market makers withdraw all support and allow the market to drop freely. Since they already have heavy short positions coupled with put options, they are not going to suffer heavy losses by acquiring some stock on the way down. The stock that is acquired is usually purchased on downside gaps. Furthermore, much of this buying is coming from covering short positions, which is the buying of stock to terminate a short position. If stock inventory is acquired, these losses can be erased quickly on the post-crash rally.

On the day of the crash, the market maker is going to wait until near the close to act. Near the close, he will begin to lend support. However, the most critical portion of specialist planning occurs on the open of trading on the following day. It usually all happens during the first hour of trading. It is during the first hour of trading on the day following a crash that the final round of sellers hit the market.

Market makers know very well that margined investors will be forced out on the open. Market makers also know that the negative publicity from the news media during the evening will panic the public into selling on the open. It is then that market makers will support the market by acquiring heavy long positions. The exact same applies to all other market makers on the other exchanges.

A crash does not necessarily signify a bear market. While the Crash of 1929 did, the Crash of 1987 did not. The circumstances were different. A crash can produce such massive accumulation at the lows that further accumulation over succeeding months may not be easily noticed. Such was the case in late 1987 and throughout 1988. In such a case, one must look at the individual stocks in order to detect further accumulation.

When the market is being advanced slowly over several months, one must look for a pattern of accumulation which is quite different from the norm. This process involves an accumulation of huge amounts of stock by exchange insiders other than specialists.

The method which is used is usually the short sale. In other words, the stock specialist will sell short the stock to other exchange insiders with the intention of covering the short on a small decline. Of course, the mutual understanding is that the specialist will hold the market and strive to advance it after a short decline. Under this process, both parties prosper, and it guarantees large blocks of stock to insiders.

When the market maker sells short to establishment insiders, a decline is to be expected. However, such a decline should be of short duration and should hold upon hitting the underlying technical support level.

One way to detect this process is merely to note the evidence of its occurrence over a period of at least two up and down cycles. The first cycle will show big block activity in some of the major stocks followed by a short decline, and the second cycle will show the same occurrence only at higher price levels. At the lows, some of the major stocks (lagging to this point) may begin to appear on the most active list. After seeing this for two or three times in a row, the analyst should conclude that the market is being advanced steadily accompanied by steady accumulation. While this steady advance takes place, the public will be exposed to negative news in order to allow the specialist to keep control during this steady process of accumulation.

The short sales figures may also provide an indication of the true situation. While specialist short sales will be high (accumulative short selling to insiders), the public short sales totals will be very high in comparison showing the high degree of public bearishness.

The short sale is not the same for all people. The specialist uses the short sale like a carpenter uses the hammer and nail. However, the public uses the short sale much like a child might use a hammer on a screw. While the specialist can make money on small declines because he constantly deals over the very short term, the public tends to hold short positions much longer because of the commission costs and lack of understanding. As a result, the public does not take advantage of small profitable moves. As the market continues to trend upward, levels of heavy public short sales become support levels until these short sellers are forced out.

A crash signifies to most investors that a bear market has begun. It is wrong to assume that a crash will lead to an economic recession or depression. For example, the crash in 1987 was not the same as the one in 1929. In October 1987, the money that was lost by those selling at the bottom was balanced by those making money by accumulation at the bottom. The accumulation process continued for one year after the crash in 1987. This accumulation led to a significant advance. One major problem with 1929 was that too many people were speculating in the market, and this could happen again. If too many people in society (including senior citizens) have their savings in stocks or mutual funds, there is a great danger that these people will remain in the market as a major portion of the decline continues. Such an occurrence could very well demolish a very large portion of the population including business concerns.

27

HISTORICAL EVIDENCE

"People of the same trade seldom meet together, even for merriment and diversion, but the conversation ends in a conspiracy against the public, or in some contrivance to raise prices." (Adam Smith, The Wealth of Nations)

Historical events are important because they tend to confirm the past. Then, once the past has been confirmed, one has to wonder if the confirmation of past events is really a confirmation that the present is no different and that the future will simply be a continuation of the past. If a politician is convicted of bribery, does it mean that maybe this sort of behavior has been going on for some time in the past with other politicians? Furthermore, does it also mean that this sort of behavior is happening in the present with other politicians? Finally, what are the odds that maybe this sort of behavior will happen into the future with other politicians?

All we have to do is to observe some of the cases that have come to light. We observe the conditions of these cases. Then, with a little common sense, we can determine what else may be going on while keeping in mind that the people that operate in the gray area of the law are able to adjust to counter the results of those legal cases. In the brokerage industry, the idea is to find ways around legal obstructions, but the problem in doing so seems to be that some people begin to abuse the loopholes until something goes wrong that may be construed as illegal by law.

The literature that follows is not just conjecture or pure editorial work. The reader should note that it can all be verified by extensive documentation found on the Internet. References are cited so that the reader may see that this work is not just a fabrication of the author. Any simple search of the Internet will reveal all of the reverences and beyond.

The Nasdaq Revelations: Tremors Begin

The commission of unethical and deceiving acts is not limited to the NYSE, nor has it been an event of recent times. The deception has gone on for decades until the Department of Justice began to take action into the 1990s based on research done by private individuals. Lucy Ackert, an economist at the Federal Reserve Bank of Atlanta, and Bryan Church, an associate professor at the Georgia Institute of Technology, present an overview of the problems encountered with the Nasdaq dealers in the following chronology.

May 24, 1994: Approximately 100 security traders meet in New York at the offices of Bear Stearns and are urged to narrow spreads.

May 26-27, 1994: Newspapers report the results of an academic study of the behavior of Nasdaq dealers by Professors William G. Christie and Paul H. Schultz. Christie and Schultz report that market makers attempt to widen spreads by avoiding odd-eighth price quotes. They conclude that the most plausible explanation for this behavior is implicit collusion. The results of the study were released to the press on May 24.

May 31, 1994: Within one week after the release of Christie and Schultz's results, dealer spreads on four prominent Nasdaq stocks narrowed, and market makers began entering odd-eighth prices quotes in those stocks. Christie, Harris, and Schultz later reported the change in behavior.

July 1994: Civil lawsuits are filed against thirty-three major dealers alleging collusion.

October 1994: The Justice Department begins an investigation of antitrust law violations.

November 1994: The SEC launches an investigation in the NASD's self-regulatory activities.

September 15, 1995: The Rudman Committee submits its report to the NASD. The NASD Board of Governors appointed the committee in November 1994 to review NASD governance and oversight structure. The committee made several recommendations intended to separate the regulatory and oversight functions of the NASD. These recommendations were later implemented.

July 17, 1996: The U.S. files a complaint alleging that twenty-four major dealers fixed prices, in violation of federal antitrust acts. The same day, the Justice Department settles with the dealers who agree to random taping of trading-desk telephone calls but neither admit nor deny wrong-doing.

August 7, 1996: The SEC concludes that the NASD violated the Exchange Act of 1934, citing deficiencies in market oversight and failure to enforce NASD and federal securities laws. In its settlement with the SEC, NASD agrees to spend $100 million over five years on additional market surveillance.

January 20, 1997: The SEC's new order-handling rules for the Nasdaq market take effect. Market makers are required for the first time to show investors the size and prices for certain orders. The SEC also directs the market to open previously exclusive electronic systems, including Instinet and SelectNet.

December 24, 1997: Thirty securities firms settle a class-action suit alleging price fixing for $910 million.

Even as all of this was taking place, there was not much fanfare in the news. For the most part, it was treated as an isolated case. Ackert and Church (1998) conclude in their report as follows, and this lends evidence to the issue that it was not an isolated case.

> The behavior of security dealers has been closely scrutinized in the 1990s. Recent investigations of the NASD and the Nasdaq market by the Justice Department and SEC suggest that prior to 1996 market makers colluded to fix prices and widen bid-ask spreads. At a minimum, market makers appeared to have adopted a quoting convention that can be viewed as anticompetitive behavior. The purpose of this practice was to increase dealers' profits at investors' expense.

These events involving the Nasdaq were slowly but surely leading up to the major event involving the stock specialists. Actually, there were many other events taking place throughout the decade that simply were never spotlighted by the media. Events of improper conduct, easily classified as legally crooked, have continued right up to the creation of this writing.

The Specialist Scandals

NYSE Rule 92 forbids specialists from entering proprietary orders when unexecuted customer orders could be executed at the same price. The two most common abuses involving the actual breaking of the law can be identified as "trading ahead" and interpositioning." While these events may be deemed illegal, they indicate that there may be much more under the surface that may be deemed legally crooked. William Christie and Robert Thompson, in an article from the Washington University Law Review, state the problem in an easy to understand format as follows.

> "Trading ahead" is a parallel behavior where the specialist exercises discretion during the few seconds available to seek price improvement for the order on the floor of the exchange. In a world characterized by investors calculating times in microseconds, this window provides a significant delay that can work in the specialists' favor. Suppose a specialist with access to the cumulative order book has observed an influx of buy orders. In the few seconds that the specialist exposed the order to price improvement on the floor of the exchange, the specialist could trade ahead of these orders, buying for the specialist's own account at a lower price and turning around and selling to the incoming buy orders at a higher price.

If you observe the wording of this carefully, you will see the possibilities that this behavior may easily be construed as taking place in the gray area of the law. There is no doubt that it is abusive behavior that can lead to fines and penalties being levied by the NYSE. However, it can be defended as not being criminal behavior that would lead to a prison sentence. However, it does constitute an act that may influence the future on following trades.

The act of "interpositioning" is illegal. This is a situation where a specialist or broker-dealer places him or herself between a buyer and seller to make a profit off their trade. While individual transactions do not amount to much, but if repeated in large volumes, this could amount to a significant loss for the investors involved on the buy or sell side of the spread. This behavior is more serious when the sum total of the damage is assessed. It can easily be seen that, because each individual happening is small, it can go on for a long period of time without being noticed. It may go on for so long that those who practice this behavior may even consider it as being part of the business.

A portion of an article written by Greg Ip, Wall Street Journal staff reporter, dated March 12, 2001, is entered here as evidence to support the claims of profitability and abuse by specialists. These statements are not taken out of context and are straight forward as follows.

The obscure functionaries who handle the murky tasks of matching buy and sell orders, keeping markets "orderly" and deciding where to "open" a stock are scoring their biggest profits ever. Profit averaged $16 million per partner in just nine months at one specialist firm last year, Spear Leeds & Kellogg. Wall Street giant Goldman Sachs Group, which had decried the NYSE floor system as a barrier to the market's competitiveness, now is rushing to acquire specialists. Phil Marber, a trader at Cantor Fitzgerald & Co., placed an order to sell 100,000 shares of Compaq for a big institutional client at no less than $24 a share. Minutes later, Mr. Marber saw a 25,000-share trade in Compaq cross the tape -- at $23.99. He called down to his broker on the floor of the New York Stock Exchange to see what happened.

Undercut by a Penny

He was told that a broker who wanted to buy 25,000 shares had entered the crowd and that the specialist firm handling Compaq stepped in and sold him shares out of the specialist's own account, for one penny less than Cantor's client was willing to sell for.

Mr. Marber says the specialist figured that with a big seller out there at $24, Compaq stock wasn't about to rally, so dumping it at $23.99 would be a good move.

148

But why didn't the specialist simply match the buy order with the Cantor client's sell order? Isn't a specialist supposed to do its own buying or selling only if there is an imbalance of buyers and sellers?

The specialist was LaBranche & Co. Its chief, Michael LaBranche, says he doesn't know this specific trade or whether his firm, in fact, sold any of the 25,000 shares. But if it did, he notes, it did the buyer a favor by selling him stock at a slightly lower price than he would otherwise get. He also says $23.99 might have better reflected supply and demand for Compaq at that moment than $24.

Critics call what LaBranche did "stepping in front" or "penny jumping," and think it's an abuse even though within the rules. "Specialists' attention to their own profit and loss risks eroding confidence in what has been a great marketplace," says Kenneth Sheinberg, head of listed-stock trading at S.G. Cowen.

But what the critics call stepping in front, specialists call "price improvement." Notes Big Board Chairman Richard Grasso: "You'll talk to people who say penny skipping is negative. You'll also talk to people who say a penny better is a penny better."

The preceding article was presented in its actual form without paraphrasing so that the reader would not be misled in any way by the author of this book. The news article clearly shows how much specialists were making at that time, and it goes further. It demonstrates how one type of abuse can be done and still be considered legal. Furthermore, and perhaps even more important, it shows how the NYSE evaluated the abuse. The mistake that was made by specialist firms becomes typical in nature. The abuse gets to be so great that it explodes. The abuse will fuel greed to the point that the events will finally lead from being legally crooked to the outright illegal. Note also that Goldman Sachs did acquire Spear Leeds & Kellogg as a subsidiary, and this should never have been allowed. However, the precedent had already been allowed with FleetBoston owning Fleet Specialists. If anything, specialist firms should have been kept completely independent of any outside ownership and influence by law.

The abuse continued which was a major mistake by the specialists. It must be the human nature quality within all of us that success breeds complacency of the rules. In early 2003, the SEC began to investigate the seven specialist firms that remained at the NYSE out of the many specialist firms that had once existed. The fact of the matter is that the consolidation of the many specialist firms into only seven becomes a major problem because the power becomes more concentrated and more prominent. Furthermore, the SEC investigation now becomes centered on just seven firms instead of the many that once existed.

Specialists have also been found guilty of, but not prosecuted for, manipulating the tick. This act is committed when a signal is given to a member of the bidding crowd to purchase only part of a public offer so that the specialist may then, in accordance with NYSE rules, buy the rest of the sell order. This process is actually legal if not done with directed conspiracy. The important thing to note in this regard is that it shows the mentality of what these people are willing to do in order to make money. It is all legal, but the mentality is crooked. It clearly shows that there exists a devious and unethical state of mind. It can only be classified as legally crooked.

Another issue termed as "freezing" also came into the picture. Freezing occurs when the specialist freezes the display book on a stock so he can first engage in trades for his own account just prior to entering the display. Then, he would execute public orders which facilitates his ability to front run and interposition.

Settlement Between SEC and NYSE

The SEC finally released the news of a settlement agreement on March 30, 2004, after about one year of investigation. The agreement included only the firms and not the individuals. The SEC official release is displayed in the Appendix as Exhibit 3. The agreement included the five specialist firms of LaBranche, Van der Moolen, Spear Leeds & Kellogg, Fleet, and Bear Wagner. These firms agreed to the payment of civil penalties and disgorgement payments toward investors that may have been hurt by the abusive behavior.

It becomes important to note that the guilty parties were really never found criminally guilty of anything. The settlement meant that the specialist firms would never go to trial. In essence, it was a payoff scam to avoid any prosecution. We can only guess what was said during those settlement talks. However, this also becomes human nature. The settlement avoided any further embarrassment to everyone involved including the government. This can easily be seen when it is considered that the ultimate responsibility did fall upon the Securities and Exchange Commission. For this case to go to trial, it would have opened up a Pandora's Box of so many problems, including not only public exposure to the truth but also the real possibility of job losses at the very top of the NYSE and SEC.

The reader should be able to realize, at this point, that being found guilty of being legally crooked is certainly not as bad as being found guilty of being illegally crooked. The paying of several million dollars for these specialist firms might just be comparable to one of us paying for a speeding ticket. Meanwhile, many individual citizens have been put in prison for doing less than the people in this case.

The David Finnerty Case

Since the initial settlement did not involve the individuals by agreement, the government now decided to take action against the employees of the firms. This event is important because it shows either the ignorant folly of the government or better still, shows that human nature amongst the people in government fits the standard. The standard for human nature, in this case, is to make it look good. In other words, if you cannot get the guys at the top, you might find it easier to go for the guys at the bottom. This is so asinine. If the firms and their leaders had been found guilty, then it would make sense to go after others for criminal prosecution. However, in this case, the firms were never found to be criminally guilty. Furthermore, most of the profits that were earned by the abuse went to the firms. This was to become just another show and another waste of government money. John Crudele (2007), of the New York Post, eloquently stated, "It's sad to know that the government still puts on these show trials so that the public thinks it's being protected without any real safeguards ever happening."

David Finnerty was a specialist at Fleet starting in 1996, and he was fired in 2003. He was often featured on CNBC and in newspaper articles concerning his views on the market. He was indicted in 2005 on charges that he had interpositioned his trades to make money for Fleet and to increase his bonuses. The U.S. Government stated that he caused investors to lose about $4.5 million. However, his attorneys defended on the grounds that it could not be demonstrated. He was initially found guilty.

In the Summer of 2008, the Court of Appeals considered the judgment of acquittal by U.S. District Court Judge Denny Chin after Finnerty's conviction. In other words, the Court of Appeals vacated the initial conviction. The contention was that investors were not hurt by the actions committed by Finnerty although it made money for the firm. It was also contended that investors received what they were expecting in the sell and the buy despite his actions. The writing was on the wall. It was another case of being legally crooked. David Finnerty and all others in the case were vindicated of all charges.

The Goldman Sachs Scandals

At this point, one has to really look at this situation with Goldman Sachs and admire the success of total and blatant arrogance. There was a time when the Federal Reserve was considered the most powerful institution in the United States. This is no longer true because power has now shifted to those who abuse power through a network of roots that are deeply embedded within the government and the media.

It becomes possible that the control establishment on Wall Street actually desires a weak United States President and a weak Congress that may be centered on progressive movements geared to the advancement of socialism for the purpose of expanding a government that is already deeply rooted with components of the investment banking control establishment. The highest probability, dictated by common sense, seems to be that the control establishment actually would not mind the complete destruction of the base foundations and moral fiber of both political parties. A more desired objective of this devious culture may be the advancement of globalization which would entail the dismantlement of national borders.

Furthermore, those who operate the control establishment must realize that its culture must be protected and reproduced within the walls of an organization.

In 2007, John Paulson, who was considered a top-of-the-line Harvard-educated hedge fund marvel with connections, asked Goldman Sachs to construct a multi-billion-dollar basket of subprime real estate investments to sell to investors. His plan was to bet against the securities by shorting since it was his opinion that the housing market was going to collapse. Goldman got a huge fee for doing the deal that became known as Abacus.

Paulson chose only those mortgages that were from borrowers with low credit ratings from states such as Florida, Arizona, Nevada, and California that represented volatile areas. The collateral manager was ACA, but the people at ACA were never informed that Paulson was short the fund. Apparently, even the people at ACA were baffled when Paulson would refuse to accept the better mortgages being offered by Wells Fargo. ACA became even more baffled when it got no satisfaction from both Goldman and Paulson.

The result, of course, is that the fund crashed in value. The SEC stated that the main problem with the deal was that Goldman never disclosed to investors the true position of Paulson's involvement. Meanwhile, Goldman Sachs tried to defend itself on the position that it was merely making a market by selling to qualified investors. In other words, Goldman Sachs had performed due diligence. This event can only be described as blatant arrogance, and more accurately described as fraud. All of this can be verified on the Internet from many sources.

Look at those who may defend Goldman Sachs, because this is very interesting. Warren Buffet, who is always being highlighted as the height of moral fiber by CNBC, implied that the fraud was the work of just one person. It turns out that Buffet held a huge amount of Goldman Sachs stock. It is also a fact that Goldman Sachs is a strong supporter of the financial media in sponsorship advertising. It is also a fact that many of the personalities featured in the media are former employees of Goldman

Sachs. It all comes together with the bottom-line being money. The media spent hours on end concerning the Madoff case, but not that much on the more serious Goldman Sachs case. In the end, Goldman Sachs will always rely on the idea that investors should be smart enough by virtue of playing the game. In other words, it is okay for Goldman Sachs to rip off qualified smart people. This has always been the mentality on Wall Street. Investors have always accepted this. As a result, this attitude has become a precedent in law. In other words, it is all legally crooked.

There were congressional hearings, and of course, Goldman Sachs held the position that it did not prosper by the event. "In my judgment, Goldman clearly misled their clients, and they misled the Congress," stated Senator Levin, Michigan Democrat, on April 13, 2011, at a press meeting. He also implied that Lloyd Blankfein, Goldman Sachs CEO, should be investigated by federal prosecutors for perjury. These events represent evidence that something is wrong with the moral fiber at this firm which is to be considered as a component of the control establishment. Although these events should be considered critical, the public is being manipulated by the media into believing that the whole affair is just a normal way of doing business.

At this point, the reader must realize that whenever an outsider is caught in a scam, the establishment must feed that person to the wolves. In other words, attention must be diverted to the outsider or possibly to a so-called rogue employee. The establishment, whether it be a private or public sector entity, must be protected at all times.

Goldman Sachs and Greg Smith

This case provides even further evidence that all that has been said has merit. This particular event is so remarkable and so awesome in nature that all of the Goldman Sachs cronies and partners in crookedness came to its aid. At this point, the reader should remember the basic principles of motivation. It all comes down to money. Of course, one must not condemn on one or two events. The problem with this investment bank is that the events tend to form a pattern over a long period of time with all the dots being connected.

On March 14, 2012, the New York Times published a letter of resignation by Greg Smith. This event comes across like an atom bomb explosion. However, the visual media, which is controlled by the establishment, has to respond immediately to give the impression that Greg Smith is nothing but an isolated case of a disgruntled employee. There is one big problem with this strategy. Greg Smith is not just a lowly common employee. He happens to be an executive director and head of the firm's United States equity derivatives business in Europe, the Middle East, and Africa.

The New York Times and Greg Smith may make some money off the reprint rights to the resignation letter. This compensation is a motivation for the newspaper to print the story. As a result, the newspaper gets the rights when a print of this nature is accepted. Everyone will always have a motive for doing something, whether it is monetary, or personal satisfaction or both.

In his resignation letter, Mr. Smith stated that the interests of the client were being sidelined by the way Goldman Sachs operates. In other words, making money for the firm has priority over the interests of the client.

28

REQUIRED MENTALITY

Never trade in the market without conviction. This means that you should not trade or invest without a resolution of the major issues that have been stated in this book regarding observed evidence of illusionary behavior. Along with this mentality comes the virtue of patience. You must be confident in your belief concerning the issues. This required mentality becomes much like a business plan from which you should not deviate. An emotional deviation from discipline will lead to ruin. It has already been shown that those who operate in the legally crooked zone of the financial world will most often allow emotional greed to overcome discipline. Therefore, the investor can only counter any of these deviant forces in the market by adhering to a disciplined plan of operation.

While investors may come in many various forms, both experienced and inexperienced traders can be reduced to financial ruin in a short period of time. The legally crooked operators of the control establishment will respect less the well-being of those who believe to be highly intelligent. To the legally crooked, the head of a lion on the wall is most certainly more valuable than that of an elk.

Experienced investors, and not just those who are starting, might do well to observe whether or not he is unconsciously succumbing to those temptations that may lead to ruin. Whenever there are successes in a row, there is a danger of complacency where a tendency develops to over-trade. This becomes the greatest curse of any investor, whether experienced or not because any ability that may have been attained will most certainly degenerate into a delusion for gambling.

When operating on a thin margin or with a high level of leverage, the smallest movement in price may make your position vulnerable. This will be especially true if you commit all of your capital to the position. You may then make the error made most often which is to rely on the hope that recovery to your entry point may occur. Whenever you find yourself clinging to a position with hope as your excuse, it is time to get out. This situation is much different from the following circumstances.

It becomes imperative to understand that markets or individual stock prices gyrate. Before a price goes in your direction, it may go against you over the very short term. If you have carefully resolved that insider activity desires a particular direction, then you should make allowances for daily gyrations in price. In other words, you should be secured with adequate margin or with reserved capital. With these precautions being taken, you really should not feel fear or receive an impulse to reverse your position unless there has been a change in the technical condition of your stock, or possibly that your original analysis of insider activity is no longer consistent with new evidence.

When using the analysis that is presented in this book, the investor must realize that the reason why a stock may drop lower may be because brokerage insiders are accumulating over a certain price range. If you notice evidence of insider accumulation at a certain level, you should look to see if there may be another technical support level just below. The range of accumulation may involve several points. If this turns out to be the case, the stock will eventually go higher well above the accumulation range. It is for this reason that it becomes appropriate to reserve capital just in case the price does go lower into a planned accumulation range.

Being patient becomes a required mentality. Entering a position too soon may be disastrous, especially if all of your capital is committed. It is human nature to desire to consummate the deal in order to maximize profit, but such a method of operation does not fit into the strategy as outlined here. Remember that the insider's range of accumulation may not be set at just one level. If the brokerage insider wants to accumulate a huge amount of stock, this may not be possible using a narrow range of price.

Becoming impatient with a position can be a problem for the undisciplined investor. It may not be easy to sit there watching other stocks go up while your stock just remains at sleep. At this point, it is human nature to be inclined to go where the action is occurring. Furthermore, it is a fact that the undisciplined investor will almost always have the anxiety to trade every day. In other words, it becomes much like a sports activity where there must be constant action. This type of undisciplined behavior will most certainly lead to disaster, and it does not fit into the philosophy of this book of which the unfolding event may involve a process of several days or weeks.

In a game of poker or chess, you must decipher the evidence of a developing situation and assume the mind of your opponent. In the marketplace, the situation becomes no different. You must develop your mentality to the point where you can detect all of the devious possibilities and conclude the probabilities. Since you already know what the insider is able to perform legally, you should be able to interject yourself onto his position.

It becomes critical that investors maintain a certain amount of convictions and beliefs concerning the market. Historical events define the future. What may have occurred in the past can happen again. Human nature does not change.

29

PRACTICE ILLUSIONALYSIS

The process of performing market maker analysis must grow on you over a period of time. It becomes an evolutionary process that improves in time. For this process to improve, it must be practiced. It is very easy since it requires only observation to start followed by the maintenance of technical charts. The only other ingredient is a clear mind void of emotional tendencies. In other words, it becomes important to understand motivations and incentives and to place oneself in the devious scenario of the group being analyzed. This type of activity must never be thought of as being a chore. It is highly interesting and satisfying. Most important of all, it is the most relevant thing you can do in the market.

You must be spiritually committed to the belief that the market maker system is a valid field of study which requires justified interpretation. You must also believe that proper interpretation can only be developed through market experience. You must always justify your conclusions and forecasts based on facts or historical reasoning. This system has nothing to do with emotional hunches or psychic phenomena. The strength of your conclusion is directly proportional to the amount of justified evidence that you can observe and collect. It must also be realized that there may be evidence which counters your conclusion. At this point, there can be no room for emotion or ego. You must always consider the evidence that goes counter to your initial conclusion and weigh that evidence against what you have. This means that you must stand ready at all times to admit that you formed a wrong conclusion either through misinterpretation or through neglect in looking at all the facts. Of course, some pieces of evidence will carry more weight than others. Students of this form of study must not become discouraged when any misjudgments are made. If all conclusions are justified, you should be correct most of the times. Never forget that the market can humble anyone.

The following should always be considered as valid evidence when evaluating market maker activity:

> block trades
> volume
> 50, 100, 200-day average lines
> Price gaps
> Technical resistance and support levels
> specialist ratios

The following should always be considered in evaluating its value as evidence at a particular point in time:

> technical support and resistance levels
> advance-decline line
> specialist tax considerations
> contrarian financial news
> movement of interest rates
> chart patterns
> number of bullish and bearish advisors
> accumulation/distribution requirements
> time and amount required
> individual Dow components

I always make it a point to tell people exactly what happens to be my greatest qualification in teaching this material. My successes in the market are secondary. One should always fear the qualifications of a teacher that are based solely on successes. My greatest qualification for being a teacher is based on my failures. It is failure that makes one strive harder and learn not to make the same mistakes again. A teacher cannot spiritually teach what has not been experienced. A teacher must convey to the student the importance of admitting failure as soon as possible and quickly make corrections. A good teacher of the market must profess that the market is capable of humbling anyone. A good teacher must also be able to admit when the path is not clear and that one should merely wait. I have found that if you expect answers every day, you will get answers that are mostly wrong.

Whenever I commit an error in judgment, I read my own book, and lo and behold; I always find that I did not follow my own word. It is important to reinforce this philosophy by continually reading this book. This book is a stock market bible with many possible avenues of thought extending from any one derivative line of thought presented.

Practice illusionalysis when considering the stock specialist system because they go together. Stock specialists and the brokerage firms that are associated with them are masters of the illusion. They can turn gold into lead and lead into gold right before your eyes. It is all done through news releases concerning upgrades and downgrades along with many other types of commentary involving deceiving future projections which carry great impact in the present but are forgotten over time. Keep in mind that it is against the code for a specialist or dealer to ever admit to any of this.

To employ this system properly, the user must make a decision based on the numbers being observed and on detective-like perceptions. Unfortunately, not many people have developed their ability to feel beyond their physical senses because this has simply never been taught in the public school system. However, with a reasonable amount of experience, anyone can learn to improve market performance and awareness by simply practicing faith in the basic concepts of the system. This should be considered a discipline of the mind which does take time to develop in practice. However, it is definitely a worthwhile cause since your wealth depends on it.

As you practice this system, your powers of accurately perceiving the market will steadily improve until you actually feel like a professional. However, despite whatever confidence you may develop, you must never feel that you have become invincible.

Every speculator should consider himself a student of the market. The learning process never ends. When involved in business, one must always keep an open mind since anything is possible. However, the most important thing is to work toward a goal which should be to become a confident decision-maker. In order to accomplish this goal, one must develop spiritual faith by truly believing that the education attained is practical, realistic and valid. One must have a market religion, a method or some sort of belief, and then one must employ all the faith possible even to have a chance to win.

Although some people may be born with "market instinct," it can be acquired through practice. This ability of spiritual mind called "market instinct" is really not a mystery at all, but is simply the ability to interpret with a fair degree of accuracy the meaning and significance of price movements and volume changes and how they relate together. In reality, it is an ability to read the trading tape intelligently. With this being true, there should be plenty of hope for anyone who is willing to study.

There is even hope for the average investor who cannot observe the action throughout the day. One can still study the daily records and charts of price changes through an electronic service.

The investor who can study the motion of the market at least once a day, and who can keep records in the form of charts along with price and volume changes, can succeed in mastering illusionalysis, market instinct or whatever you may wish to call it. In order to form an accurate interpretation, one must maintain charts of favorite issues and of the general market averages.

There is nothing mysterious about this study. The ability to interpret market information is available to anyone who is willing to observe the market. It will take time, and much may come through actual experience. If one is not willing to do a serious study, then the game will surely revert back to the status of gambling. Speculation does involve a fair degree of analysis. Speculation may also involve a fair degree of intuition. However, gambling may be just a matter of intuition on the throw of a pair of dice.

From prior reading in this book, the reader already knows that every stock is either under accumulation, under distribution, or in a movement between these two phases, or possibly in limbo without interest from anyone. A stock investment must never be made unless one can determine with some justification in which phase the stock is situated.

There is one very important final note concerning this practice. This is critical to your success. There will be times when the path ahead of us becomes obscure. At this point, we must learn to practice keeping control of anxiety and being patient. In other words, there will be times when we must do nothing in the market and simply wait for the path to clear. Do nothing unless you see clearly the evidence of what is occurring. Learn to be patient in such cases. Just as it is true in nature, the fog always disappears with the passage of time. Expect this to happen and consider it part of your discipline.

There is simply no need to chase rainbows which are in reality nothing but illusions of the eye. However, it is important to know that there are rainbows in the market just as in nature. The rainbows that are produced in the market are geared to attract you into following the bright colors to the legendary pot of gold. Just remember that all rainbows are automatically geared to disintegrate over a very short period of time. Illusions are legal because they appear in the surrounding context of reality, but the illusion that may be purposely devised is most certainly crooked. It is meant to deceive.

CONCLUSION

In the present work, the state of being legally crooked is associated with the stock market. However, the mentality of deception and illusion can be applied to many other issues in life. It can be applied to the objectives of a prosecutor, a news commentator, the creator of a news report, the operator of a research study, the manager of a political survey, and perhaps a player in a game of poker. The objective is to deceive according to the motivations of the operator. The state of being legally crooked is universal.

It is highly unlikely that the control establishment system will change in basic concept. The market maker influence is much more powerful than what people realize or are led to believe. As long as the market making department remains as a profitable arm of each major investment banking establishment, major reforms will be kept to a minimum. Furthermore, any congressional investigation will end as it always has ended. It becomes the conclusion of this book that we should not waste time fighting the system but should instead learn as much as possible about the system. Therefore, investors should make use of this knowledge to better themselves in the market.

It is totally naïve to think that the NYSE and Nasdaq would install computerized market makers to assume the duties of trading. Anyone who implies that such a thing is possible does not comprehend the power nor the true fiber of those who operate these major exchanges. The character of exchange insiders as portrayed in this book is not limited to one nation. It is found on every worldwide exchange. For that reason, the work that is found in this book is valid all over the world.

Some people may contend that nationalization or more federal control is the cure. These actions would only make matters worse. The only thing that would change is that the government would now be even more guilty of being legally crooked. We would only end up with a system that was just as crooked but would also become less efficient.

First, it is only proper that specialist and all market maker activity be reported to the public on a more current basis. A second step to this would be to report specialist and all other market maker activity for each stock. Of course, the specialist would contend that he has a right to privacy. Furthermore, the NYSE would most likely contend that the cost of such reporting could not be justified and that the information would be of no value to the public. In reality, such information would be of more value than all the numbers reported by the government and Federal Reserve. As far as privacy is concerned, the specialist should have none since he is trading according to his knowledge of the public's positioning of buy and sell orders. Knowing the bulk of the buy and sell orders at various price levels represents the greatest threat to the public good. Furthermore, he also receives insider knowledge not available to the public.

The main problems are not as easily solved and would require congressional action since it is certain that the NYSE would never act on its own to change the present balance of power. The real problem is connected with the legal capability of the specialist and other market makers to trade on inside information. Knowing news releases and other relevant information prior to public release represents a big portion of the problem that should be addressed. Of course, the U.S. Congress is becoming more and more reluctant to touch the issue of doing market investigations, because of the involvement of government already in the market better known as the Securities and Exchange Commission.

Releasing information to a stock specialist or any other type of market maker prior to public release should be outlawed in every sense of the word. It is totally repulsive to the moral meaning of "government by the people" to exempt a select few (who stand to profit) from a law which governs the people as a whole. In no way should a specialist be allowed to have access to confidential corporate decisions or to maintain any sort of confidential communication with any of the corporate directors. Furthermore, it is even questionable whether it is ethical for brokerage firms to hold positions on a board-of-directors. Once a brokerage firm with market maker capabilities has a board seat, it should be quite obvious what will occur. Even an uneducated peasant from a third world country knows what the end result will be. Under the present law, there are simply too many ways for confidential information to transfer from the corporation to the operators of the stock market system. While the public cannot trade on such information nor even have access to it, there are a select few who are legally able to use it. The evidence is quite decisive. When the homing pigeons carrying information are released, they all come to roost at the doors of the major brokerage houses. As unethical as all this may seem, the securities industry will always justify the system by stating that it is all geared for the public good in true dedication toward the maintenance of efficient markets.

The market strategist that uses the concept of market maker analysis and block-volume reversal will be using the most valid and lasting method of all those philosophies being used. This conclusion is based on the fact that market makers are the smartest of all stock market traders. The material to support this system of analysis will always be present. If the user of this art form is ever wrong, it is because he or she failed to interpret the evidence properly. Even if the reader believes in other methods of analysis, the information in this book can be used as a supplement to confirm any other method being used.

To do well in the market, one should have a fair amount of fundamental knowledge and an enormous amount of psychological awareness. This type of awareness or market instinct is the most important and most critical of decision tools. People who only depend on traditional facts to make decisions are in for a shock in the stock market. In reality, the majority of speculators happen to be people who base their decisions according to the traditional learning as received from the media, book publishers and the traditional educational system. As a result of this type of learning, the majority of people lose.

People have spent their lives being taught the rules that they should play by. This programming process begins in the first grade, and it continues through high school. People are never taught that in life there is always an opponent who operates under a modified set of rules. Our education system fails to teach people about the opponent. In general, people are not very well prepared to understand the business of dealing with other people. In the market, one's opponents are more skilled and possess greater control of the game. Therefore, in order to combat such an opponent, one must study the opponent's game-style. These are issues that are not considered necessary by the public school system. Government agencies are so oblivious to reality that a spearheaded, covert movement could easily take over key elements of the government.

Traditional analysis, which involves making a decision based on economic fundamentals, totally ignores the existence of manipulation, and it certainly does not take into account the existence of stock specialists and other market makers. The traditional theory that is taught in our schools does not even recognize that there are established entities operating in the gray area of the law. Since most people operate according to fundamentals, this is used as a weapon against the public because of the public's predictability.

Brokerage market makers, followed by other types of smart money elements, represent the force that is the core of true contrarianism which is to do the opposite of what the majority of investors is doing. In reality, the specialist trader is the orchestrator of contrarianism. However, although many people believe in contrarianism, the specialist trader is not really recognized as being the cause of contrary price movements.

People do not seem to realize that the market is an artificial creation which is run by human incentives and is not a self-run system of nature. They do not seem to believe that there must be a reason and a motive for a contrary price movement to occur. They have not learned that the stock market, just like a gambling casino, represents a flow of capital from the public to the operators. There is a mutual relationship between the specialists and the exchange establishment. In other words, what is good for the specialist must also be good for the exchange. Money must flow inward in order for the operation to be operated so efficiently.

Contrarian philosophy is valid because there is intervention by the exchange insider whose motive is making money. Contrary price movement occurs because the stock specialist must buy when the public sells heavily and must sell when the public buys heavily, all of which gives the specialist the incentive to reverse the movement adopted by the public. In order to reverse the movement, the stock operator will oversupply at the top and will absorb supply at the bottom.

It is imperative that one comprehend the concept of Machiavellian power which is the exertion of control through the use of persuasion, if not deceit and manipulation. In any educational system, people are not taught Machiavellian principles, because such principles imply something negative about political power. It is simply not patriotic to think in such terms concerning the political establishment. As a result, the majority of people are not prepared to cope with deceit nor are they prepared to recognize manipulation.

Many people believe that Machiavellian practices are immoral or illegal. This general belief certainly accounts for the lack of teaching on this subject in the schools. However, people fail to realize that there are varying degrees of deceit and manipulation. Some forms are outlawed by regulation while others are not. In the market, there are regulations governing manipulation and insider trading. Most every investor has been taught through the news media concerning the law and has been brainwashed into believing that no one is exempt. Yet, there are exemptions.

The art of smart money analysis is based on the actions of those people who are exempt from the laws restricting insider information. The key to the system is to comprehend the motivational behavior of those elite few who fall into this category. Successful diagnosis should include the concept that smart money people are capable of widespread manipulation through deception while in possession of nonpublic information.

The material presented in this book is meant to be a series of basic concepts. It is up to the intelligent speculator to make proper use of the concepts and to apply them to any situation that may arise. Knowing the basic concepts of specialist activity will most always be helpful but cannot be maximized unless one is willing to apply interpretation which relates the concepts with current conditions and occurrences in the market. The basic principles in this work will apply in bullish and bearish markets because the market maker will always use established techniques to maximize capital no matter if in a bull or a bear market.

From each of the many lines of thought presented in this book, the reader may very well find many avenues of applications suitable for any particular situation. Once the investor knows the mentality of the exchange insider, he will be able to apply himself to many situations not covered in a book. You must possess a dual mind. You must think as your own person, and you must also be able to think as your opponent as you go through time under varying economic conditions.

In the final illusionalysis, it becomes important to observe how all of the parts are related and interacted upon. Each of the major brokerage houses possesses analysts that cover certain stocks and possess market makers that deal in certain stocks. Then, it must be considered that the media receives input from the major houses which may also be sponsors of the media. It must also be considered that the futures can easily be influenced by targeted trading during the night. Finally, it must be considered that many exchange insiders are on the boards of some of the largest companies. The only possible common-sense conclusion to all of this must be that market dealers will, whenever opportunities exist, act against the welfare of investors. With so much information being acquired by people that are so inter-related can only mean that the opportunity for collusion is a reality. Although it is all accepted as being legal, it should be recognized by anyone of normal intelligence that it certainly cannot be considered ethical or moral. It represents deviant behavior that can only be described as being crooked.

Critics of this book may take things out of context, which is to be expected. Furthermore, critics may say, as they once did, concerning the specialists, that these market operators are only doing their job under the close eye of the government. The fact remains that critics cannot dispute human nature. The ultimate truth about human nature is that the urge to seek power in the financial and political sense becomes paramount.

This writer will dispute anyone who tries to take context out of the main theme. The main theme of this work is that the control establishment complex, comprised of the major brokerage houses, key government

169

agencies, and upper management of corporations, operates under a system of being legally crooked. Beyond the theme of this work, the objective is to inform the investor of the real picture that is so purposely hidden by the illusion that is so purposely created by those in financial power who are reinforced by those in political power.

The reader, as a member of the jury of readers, should now review the evidence as presented in the Exhibits and in the References. The reader should apply as much deliberation as possible from both views, one being that all that has taken place and is taking place is simply business as usual, or that something is seriously going in the wrong direction with a deviant intent to control the general population. It is contended here that the defendant, the Control Establishment Complex, is composed of people who firmly believe that the wrong direction is really the right direction and that deviant behavior is just business as usual.

You have now heard all of the major evidence, and this book now rests on the evidence and reasoning within. The defense, represented as the Control Establishment Complex, will rest on its 5th Amendment rights. After due deliberation, how do you, the jury of readers, find the accused, guilty or not guilty on the charge of being legally crooked?

REFERENCES

Ackert, L. F. & Church, B. K. (1998). Competitiveness and price setting in dealer markets. *Economic Review.* Third quarter, 1998. Federal Reserve Bank of Atlanta.

Agrawal, A. & Chen, M. (2005). Analyst conflicts and research quality. University of Alabama and University of Maryland.

Angel, J. J. (1997). Short selling on the NYSE. Washington, D.C.: Georgetown University.

Benediktsdottir, S. (2006). An empirical analysis of specialist trading behavior at the New York Stock Exchange. *International Finance Discussion Papers.* Board of Governors of the Federal Reserve System.

Blau, B., Van Ness, B. & Van Ness, R. (2011). Information in short selling: Comparing Nasdaq and the NYSE. *Review of Financial Economics.* Elsevier, Inc.

Boehmer, E., Saar, G. & Yu, L. (2004). Lifting the veil: An analysis of pretrade transparency at the NYSE. *The Journal of Finance.*

Bowlin, L. & Rozeff, M.S. (1987). Do specialists' short sales predict returns? *The Journal of Portfolio Management.* Spring 1987, Vol. 13, No. 3: pp. 59-63.

Bureau of Labor Statistics. http://www.bls.gov/cps/cps_htgm.htm#data

Clarke, J., Khorana, A., Patel, A. & Rau, P. (2009). Independents' day? Analyst behavior surrounding the Global Settlement. Social Science Electronic Publishing.

Christie, W. G. & Thompson, R. B. (2006). Wall street scandals: The curative effects of law and finance. *The Washington University Law Review.* Vol. 84, Number 7, 2006.

Chung, D. & Hrazdil, K. (2010). Liquidity and market efficiency: Analysis of Nasdaq firms. *Global Finance Journal.* 21, 262-274.

Chung, K. & Cho, S. (2005). Security analysis and market making. *Journal of Financial Intermediation.* Elsevier, Inc.

Crudele, J. (2007). How feds messed up their specialists' case. *New York Post.* February 27, 2007. Posted on nypost.com.

Cushing, D. & Madhavan, A. (2000). Stock returns and trading at the close. *Journal of Financial Markets.* Vol. 3, Issue 1, February 2000.

Engelen, P. & Liedekerke, L. (2007). The ethics of insider trading revisited. *Journal of Business Ethics.* Dordrecht, Netherlands: Springer Science & Business Media.

Harris, L. E. (1996). Does a large minimum price variation encourage order exposure? Unpublished manuscript, University of Southern California.

Irvine, P.J.A. (2001). Do analysts generate trade for their firms? Evidence from the Toronto stock exchange. *Journal of Accounting and Economics.* Elsevier Science.

Jegadeesh, N. & Kim, W. (2004). Value of analyst recommendations: International evidence.

Madhavan, A. (2002). Market microstructure: A practitioner's guide. *Financial Analysts Journal.* Charlottesville, US: CFA Institute.

Madhavan, A., Porter, D. & Weaver, D. (2000). Should securities markets be transparent? Unpublished manuscript, University of Southern California.

Madhavan, A. & Smidt, S. (1992). An analysis of daily changes in specialist inventories and quotations. Philadelphia, PA: University of Pennsylvania, Rodney L. White Center for Financial Research.

Manne, H. G. (1966). *Insider trading and the stock market.* Free Press, New York.

McGee, R. W. (2007). Applying ethics to insider trading. *Journal of Business Ethics.* Dordrecht, Netherlands: Springer Science & Business Media.

Michaely, R. & Womack, K. (1999). Conflict of interest and the credibility of underwriter analyst recommendations. Oxford University Press.

Michaely, R. & Womack, K. (2007). What are analysts really good at?

Neill, H. (2001). *The Art of Contrary Thinking.* Caldwell, Idaho: Caxton Press.

Ney, R. (1970). *The wall street jungle.* New York: Grove Press, Inc.

Ney, R. (1974). *The wall street gang.* New York: Avon Books, Division of Hearst Corp.

Ney, R. (1975). *Making it in the market.* New York: McGraw-Hill Company.

Robbani, M. & Bhuyan, R. (2005). Introduction of futures and options on a stock index and their impact on the trading volume and volatility: Empirical evidence from the DJIA components. *Journal of Derivatives & Hedge Funds.* London, UK: Palgrave Macmillan.

Schultz, P. (2003). Who makes markets. *Journal of Financial Markets*. Elsevier Science B.V.

Small Business Authority, (2011). US GDP -- Target of deception. *Entrepreneurs*. Retrieved from http://www.forbes.com. Published 8/30/2011.

Smith, Adam, (1776). *An inquiry into the nature and causes of the wealth of nations*. Reprint, 1994. New York: Modern Library.

Theissen, E. (2000). Market structure, informational efficiency and liquidity: An experimental comparison of auction and dealer markets. *Journal of Financial Markets*. 3, 333-363.

Torngren, G. and Montgomery, H. (2004). Worse than chance? Performance and confidence among professionals and laypeople in the stock market. *The Journal of Behavioral Finance*. The Institute of Psychology and Markets.

Williams, W. J. (2004). Government economic reports: Things you've suspected but were afraid to ask! Gross domestic product. *Shadow Government Statistics*. Retrieved from http://www.shadowstats.com.

ADDENDUM

The limited exhibits that are presented here are meant to support the presentation of, "Legally Crooked." The ones presented here are really meant to give the reader more perspective of this whole affair to support the thesis that the work presented in this book is not just a conspiracy theory. Because of copyright laws, much of this is paraphrased.

(Note: The reader should realize the difference in timeframe from this printing to the present time of this reading. The principle does not change. Human motivations do not change.)

Exhibit 1: Example Charts

The following composite of charts may be helpful in illustrating some of the situations presented in this work. It must be understood from the start that not all chart formations will conform nicely to any set formulas. It becomes a matter of sorting through the charts of many stocks in order to recognize those peculiarities that give away the intrusions of the market makers. While tracking the behavior of specialists on an intra-day basis is of critical importance, the second best method is to study their tracks on the charts. Price movement, volume, channel lines, W formations, gaps, and support and resistance lines are all interactions of the market maker.

The charts were acquired from TeleChart 2000 by a promotional agreement. The graphic trendlines and analysis were created by Anthony Campos.

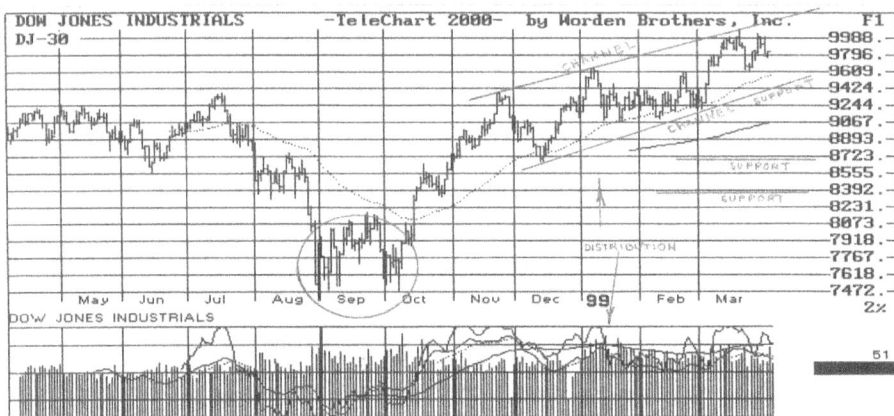

DOW JONES INDUSTRIALS   -TeleChart 2000-   by Worden Brothers, Inc.

In the circle, we see an example of a "W" formation with the two lows occurring about five weeks apart. It can also be seen that volume was heavy on both occasions. On the second decline, there was widespread fear that the Dow would drop another thousand points. I issued a buy recommendation on the second decline. Knowing about the specialist mentality caused me to consider certain factors not talked about in the mainstream. I stated that specialists had already accumulated plenty of stock because of panic selling. Furthermore, I also stated that specialists did not want to cause irreparable damage to the mutual funds. In other words, exchange insiders did not want to kill those who transport the supply of capital into the market. A further indication was that many Dow stocks were already showing up trends when the second decline occurred.

To the right on the chart, an uptrend channel developed. If the channel is broken to the downside, the market would then be subject to the support lines which are drawn. There was some distribution in January, but it was not major as can be seen on the chart.

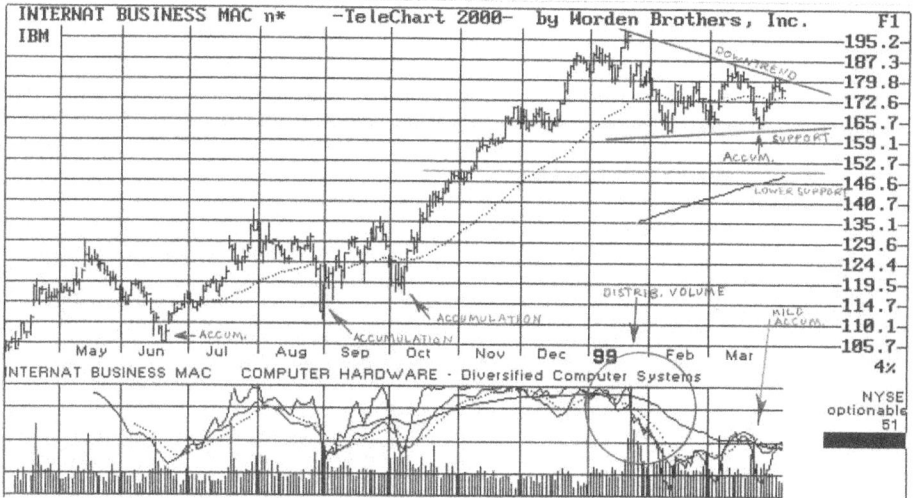

The volume has always been important for IBM at tops and bottoms. Higher than normal volume detected accumulation in June, late August, and early October. Then volume remained fairly low until January where distribution occurred as IBM hit the 199 level. To the right side of the chart, the situation turns bearish with the formation of a downtrend line. However, it is not extremely bearish because the lower channel line is tilted upward. If the channel line is broken to the downside, then the lower support line at the 149 level becomes the target. As can be seen, evidence of accumulation is weak except for a small amount at the lows in March. If the line is broken to the upside, then it should rally to prior highs.

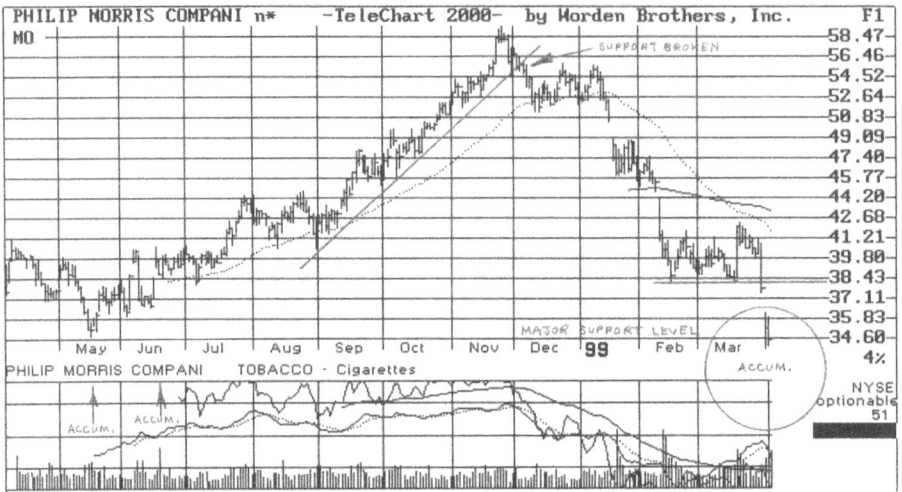

Here is an example of a tumbling, major Dow component. The first sign of accumulation was at the 38 level with a side movement. Major accumulation with extremely heavy volume and a gap occurred to the right of the chart. It was taken to the May lows. The gap should be expected to be filled over the intermediate term. The buying of put options rose to an extreme level. It should also be expected that a base formation should occur between 32 and 38 to allow for further accumulation by the specialist.

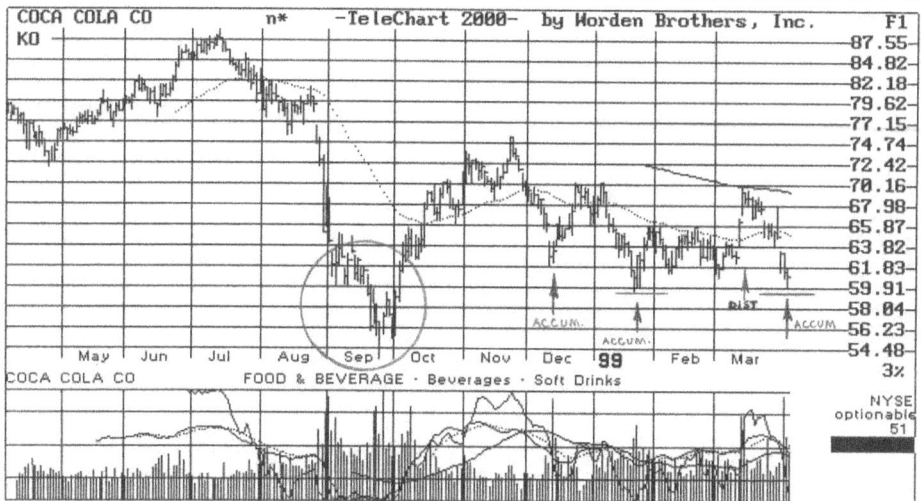

COCA COLA CO n* —TeleChart 2000— by Worden Brothers, Inc. F1

Accumulation was quite heavy in the September period. Coke had already come off its record high in July. Here is a case of a prolonged period of several months in which the stock is merely being steered up and down by the specialist with accumulation occurring on every major decline. Eventually, this stock will be taken back up to prior highs. Accumulation is occurring at the 59-61 range.

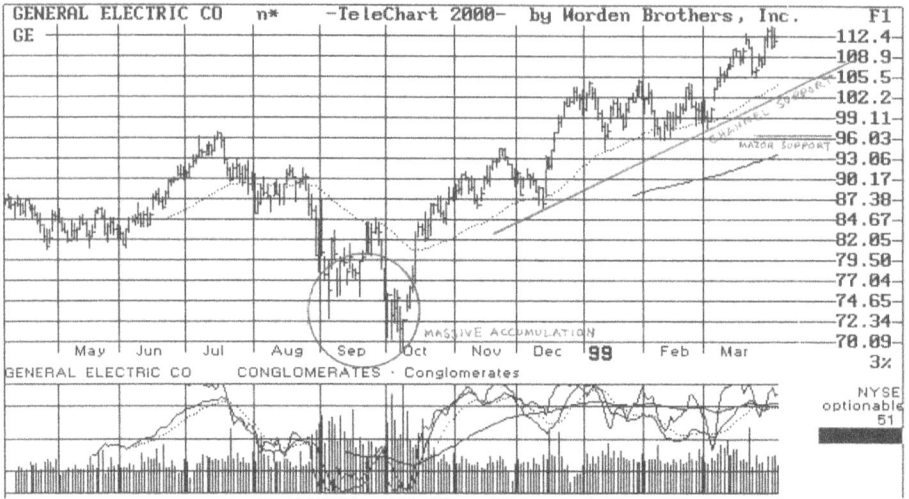

GENERAL ELECTRIC CO   n*   -TeleChart 2000-   by Worden Brothers, Inc.

Massive accumulation occurred in September and October. There is no sign of major distribution which means that insiders are most likely going for a one year hold for tax purposes. You should always draw the lower channel support line and then draw the horizontal support lines as pictured here. Now and then, the specialist will take the price down to the channel support line to cover short positions and accumulate more shares as seems to be the case here.

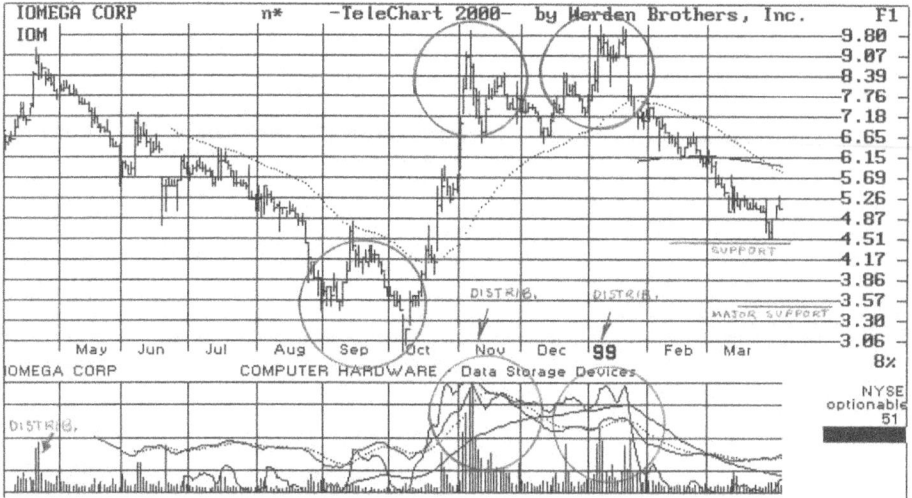

IOMEGA CORP   n*   -TeleChart 2000-   by Worden Brothers, Inc.   F1

The "W" formation is the only positive since accumulation was weak. In this chart, it is distribution that is the dominating factor. Distribution was massive over two different occasions. As can be seen, volume was very heavy in November and in January. A configuration of distribution such as this is basic in specialist analysis. This stock should have been sold without question in early November upon seeing the volume line rising. Without any further evidence of accumulation, this stock should not be bought unless volume rises on declines to support levels or should there occur a bullish, bottom formation.

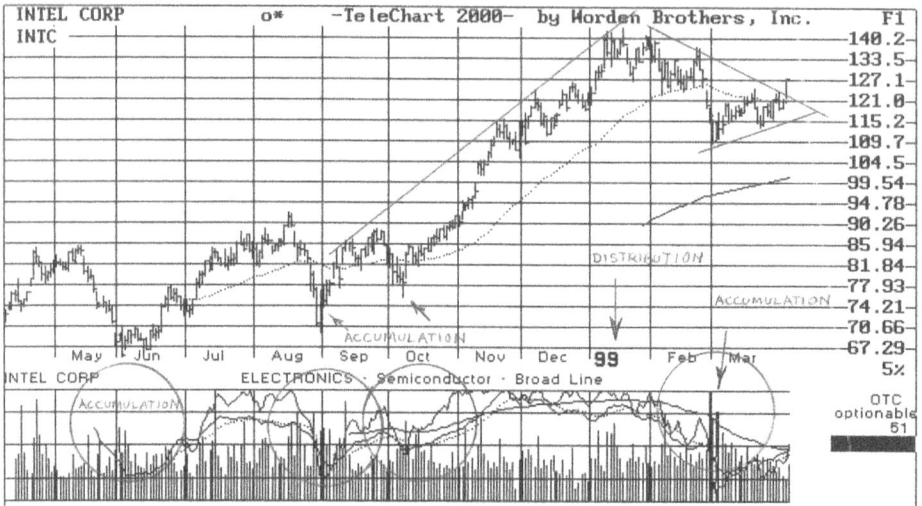

INTEL CORP   o*   —TeleChart 2000— by Worden Brothers, Inc.   F1
INTC

In the period from June to October, accumulation occurred at every low. Although there was a fair degree of distribution in January, major accumulation occurred again in early March. From January to early April, we see an upper downtrend line with a lower uptrend support line. With no sign of distribution and with a breakout to the upside, the Intel market maker wants to go higher to prior highs.

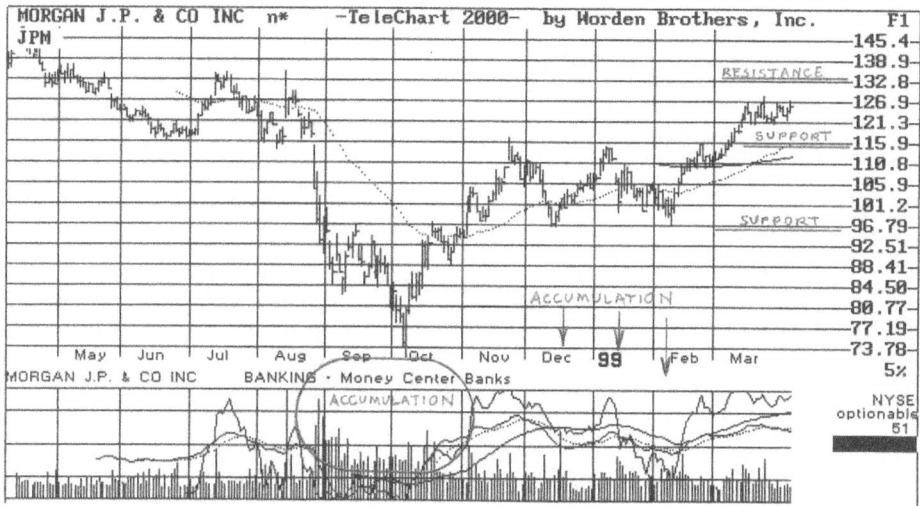

MORGAN J.P. & CO INC   n*   -TeleChart 2000-   by Worden Brothers, Inc.   F1

Here is an example of obvious, heavy accumulation through September and October. Most of it occurred between 84 and 88. Accumulation occurred again at each low in December, January, and February. There is no sign of distribution which means that exchange insiders are going for a one-year holding period. This specialist wants the price much higher by the following October.

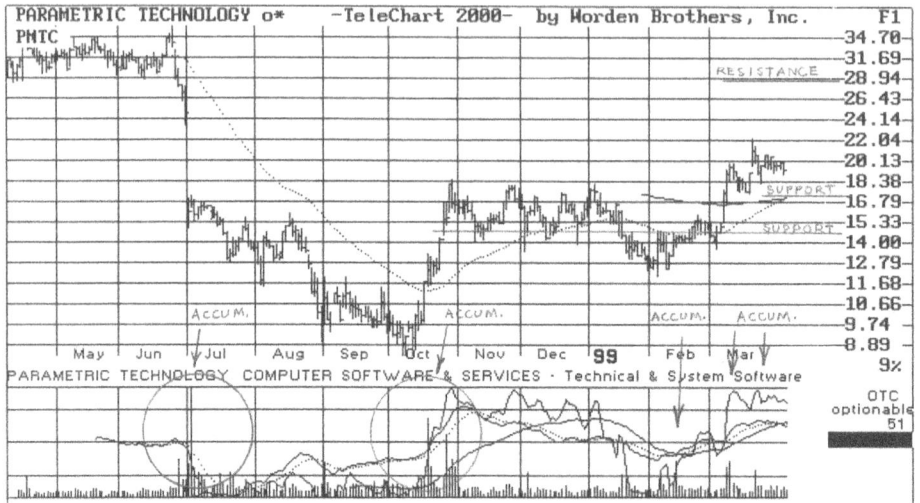

PARAMETRIC TECHNOLOGY o*   —TeleChart 2000—   by Worden Brothers, Inc.   F1

Here is an example of a battered stock under the threat of lawsuits. There is evidence of continual accumulation throughout its basing process from July to February. Although this type of accumulation is drawn out over a long period of time, those insiders who invest are highly rewarded with up to a 200 percent return over a period of one year.

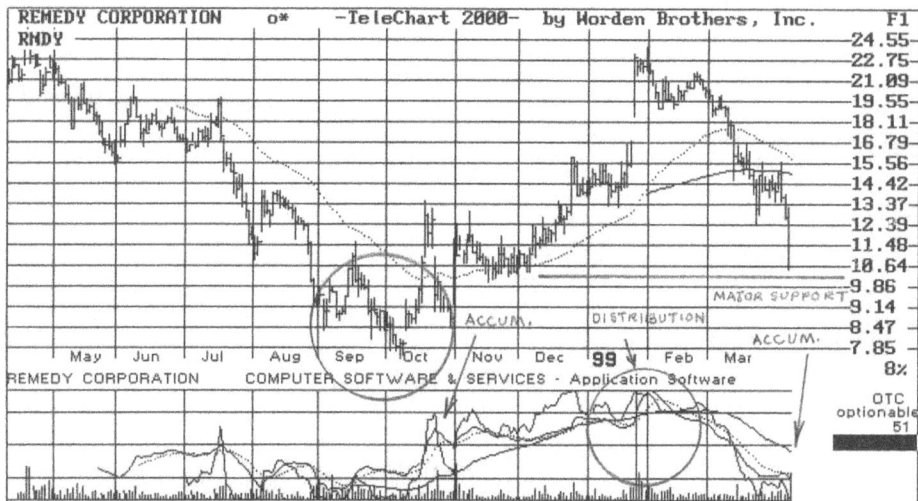

REMEDY CORPORATION   o*   -TeleChart 2000-   by Worden Brothers, Inc.   F1
RMDY
REMEDY CORPORATION   COMPUTER SOFTWARE & SERVICES - Application Software

     Here is an example of a reverse head and shoulders formation (very bullish). As may be true with many low cap stocks, heavy volume may not be evident at bottoms. Therefore, the bottom formation and the following uptrend line tells the story. The only problem occurred on the heavy volume advance in late January. That advance was negative because it signified a fair amount of distribution by the market makers to the public on the high demand. At this point, the market makers knew that the interest was there. They had a winner that had reached its limit. The stock was most likely heavily shorted by brokerage insiders. At this point, the key to the future is the downward spike on heavy volume which is unfolding at the right end of the chart. It is dropping right down to a major support level. This is a prime example of what the investor should be looking for. The market makers are forcing all those on margin to sell at those lows. When those on margin are selling their long positions, the market makers are covering their short positions on increased volume. The main point to get out of this chart is that you should consider selling if in a long position on an upward spike accompanied by heavy volume after a prolonged advance.

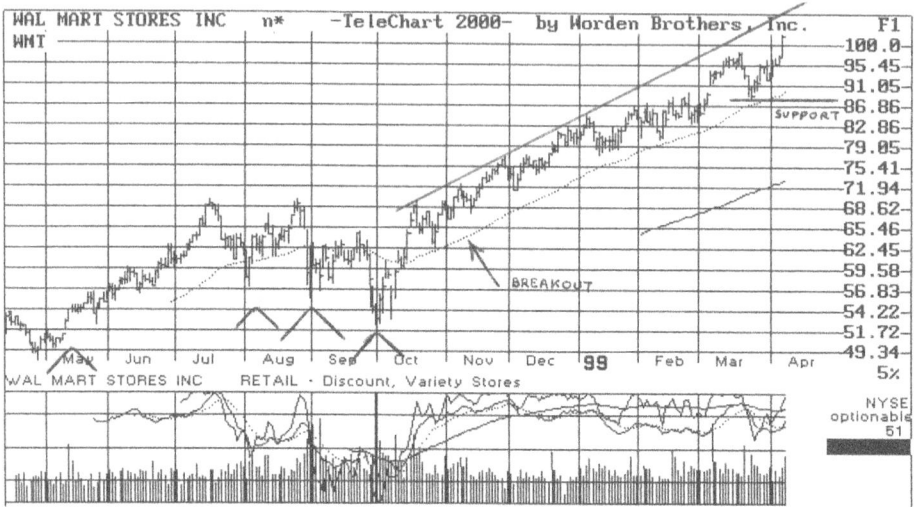

WAL MART STORES INC   n*   —TeleChart 2000—   by Worden Brothers, Inc.   F1
WMT

Price scale (right axis): 100.0, 95.45, 91.05, 86.86, 82.86, 79.05, 75.41, 71.94, 68.62, 65.46, 62.45, 59.58, 56.83, 54.22, 51.72, 49.34, 5%

Months (bottom axis): May, Jun, Jul, Aug, Sep, Oct, Nov, Dec, '99, Feb, Mar, Apr

SUPPORT

BREAKOUT

WAL MART STORES INC   RETAIL · Discount, Variety Stores

NYSE
optionable
51

Here is an example of a popular stock that encountered some form of accumulation on every decline over a period of six months before the breakout to the upside. This demonstrates that major accumulation by exchange insiders on a quality stock does take time. There is no sign of distribution on this chart. However, its six-month rise could encounter trouble on any advance to the rising trendline. A decline should then be expected to the line of support. Note that accumulation was very strong in late September and early October. Considering the one year holding period for tax purposes, this issue should be close to its highs by the following September despite any corrections.

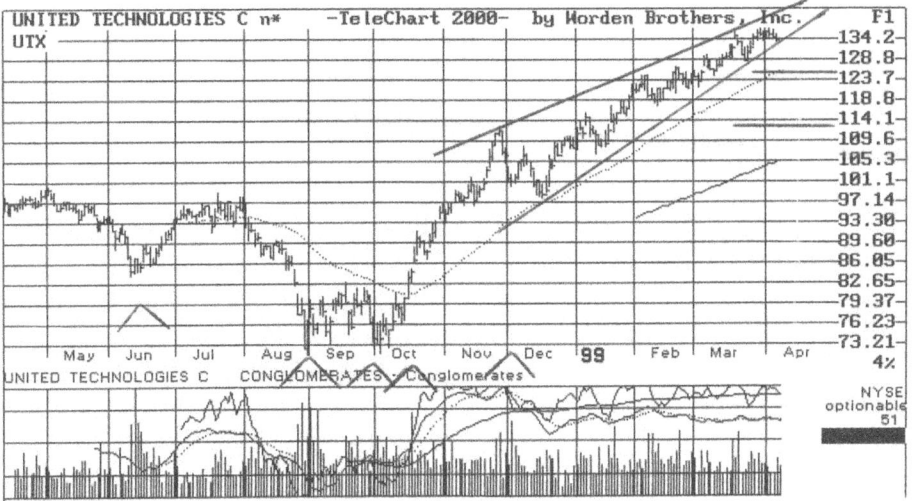

UNITED TECHNOLOGIES C n*   —TeleChart 2000— by Worden Brothers, Inc.

Here we see the familiar "W" formation along with accumulation at every low. Note that the upper and lower trendline is forming an apex to the right. There is a good probability that a correction could occur from that apex. The lines of support are drawn. However, major distribution has not yet occurred on this chart. If a major correction does occur, the support at 114 should hold if further accumulation occurs. This chart does suggest that exchange insiders have accumulated for a one-year holding period. In seven months, this Dow issue has advanced by over 90%.

Exhibit 2: The Crash of 1987

The chart of the crash of 1987 will always be of interest and is being presented here as a historical reference. No one could predict the enormity of this event although there was evidence of a normal decline. Only a few days before the crash, there was evidence that specialists were shorting. The chart formation was normal leading into October 9th. You will note that lines A and B formed the down channel while lines B and C formed the beginning of a broadening formation. In other words, the normal thing to happen would have been for line B to hold. Then the expectation would have been for the market to break out above line A which would then place the resistance at line C (the objective).

Now look at line B. The Dow broke below the channel line on increasing volume. This meant that accumulation was not taking place. Specialists were not holding the market where they normally would accumulate. No one may never know the real reason except for the specialists themselves. Something must have kept them from covering their short positions. Perhaps it had something to do with what they saw in their books. Perhaps there were simply too many sell orders being entered onto the books. It is possible that specialists were simply not planning for any major accumulation at the 2420 level. There is a chance that they were planning for another low a little later in the year. Whatever the case may have been, they made no move to accumulate at a point where they normally would have initiated a rally. As can easily be seen, the volume kept increasing into an area of no technical support. Specialists simply refused to step in once the market broke well below line B.

Over the following few months, line E marked the area of resistance, and line D became the channel support. It was evident that the 1940 level had become solid equilibrium. There were more steady signs of accumulation by the end of November and in through December. The triangular pattern on the chart of exhibit 2 is a very bullish pattern. You will see this pattern on the charts of many stocks. It is flat across the top with an upward slanting bottom line. This pattern is bullish. The Dow divisor was .754. With the present divisor, the crash would have involved well over 2500 points. (Note: Depending on the time of this reading, the crash could well involve much more in Dow points.)

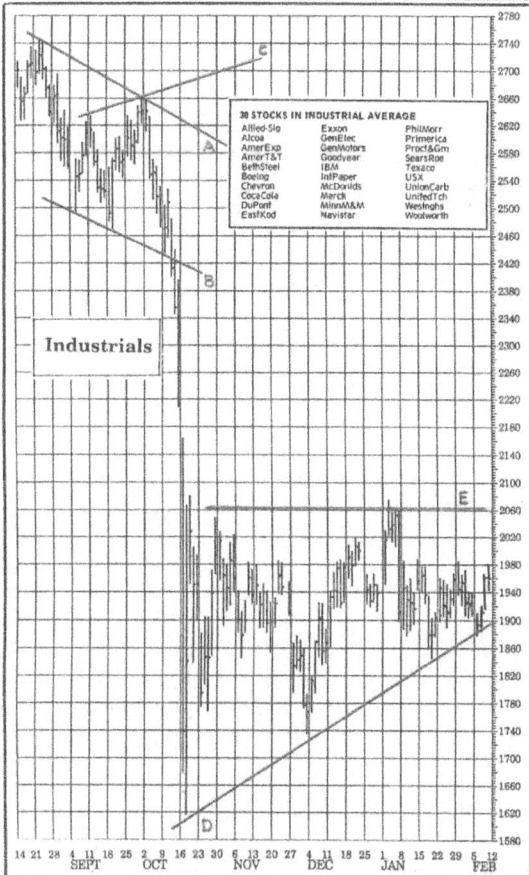

30 STOCKS IN INDUSTRIAL AVERAGE		
Allied-Sig	Exxon	PhilMorr
Alcoa	GenElec	Primerica
AmerExp	GenMotors	Proct&Gm
AmerT&T	Goodyear	SearsRoe
BethSteel	IBM	Texaco
Boeing	IntPaper	USX
Chevron	McDonlds	UnionCarb
CocaCola	Merck	UnitedTch
DuPont	MinnM&M	Westnghs
EastKod	Navistar	Woolworth

Industrials

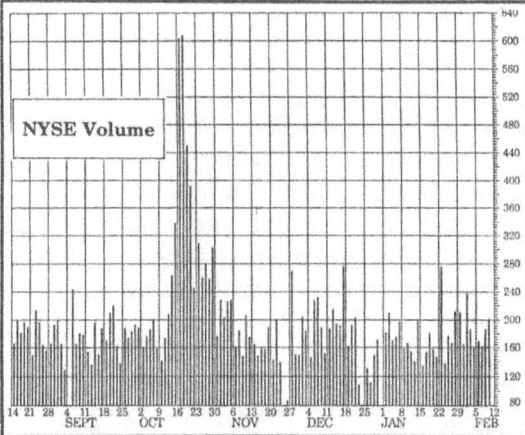

NYSE Volume

Exhibit 3: SEC Specialist Settlement

Settlement Reached With Five Specialist Firms for Violating Federal Securities Laws and NYSE Regulations; Firms Will Pay More Than $240 Million in Penalties and Disgorgement

FOR IMMEDIATE RELEASE
2004-42

Firms Will Pay More Than $240 Million in Penalties and Disgorgement

Washington, D.C., Mar. 30, 2004 -- The U.S. Securities and Exchange Commission and the New York Stock Exchange today announced the initiation and settlement of enforcement actions against five NYSE specialist firms. The firms will pay a total of $241,823,257 in penalties and disgorgement, consisting of $87,735,635 in civil money penalties and $154,087,622 in disgorgement, and implement steps to improve their compliance procedures and systems. The five settling specialist firms are: Bear Wagner Specialists LLC; Fleet Specialist, Inc.; LaBranche & Co., LLC; Spear, Leeds & Kellogg Specialists LLC; and Van der Moolen Specialists USA, LLC.

In a joint investigation, the NYSE and SEC found that, between 1999 and 2003, the five firms, through particular transactions by certain of their registered specialists, violated federal securities laws and Exchange rules by executing orders for their dealer accounts ahead of executable public customer or "agency" orders. Through these transactions, the firms violated their basic obligation to match executable public customer buy and sell orders and not to fill customer orders through trades from the firm's own account when those customer orders could be matched with other customer orders. Through this conduct, the firms improperly profited from trading opportunities; disadvantaged customer orders, which either received inferior prices or went unexecuted altogether; and breached their duty to serve as agents to public customer orders. In the settlements, the firms have neither admitted nor denied the allegations.

Stephen M. Cutler, the SEC's Director of Enforcement, said, "When an exchange specialist unlawfully takes advantage of its privileged position by seizing trading opportunities that it should leave for public customers, it fundamentally undermines the fair and orderly operation of the exchange auction system. As the sanctions imposed in this case indicate, the Commission will aggressively punish such conduct."

"The terms of this settlement are appropriate, and tell the investing public, specialists and all market participants that violations of NYSE rules and federal securities laws will not be tolerated," said Marshall N. Carter, NYSE director and chairman of the NYSE's Regulatory Oversight and Regulatory Budget Committee. "Confidence in the integrity of our market is paramount. I am confident that the imposed sanctions and requirements for specialist firms to improve their own oversight and compliance functions will help deter future violative activity."

The settlement provides that the firms' $241 million payment will go to a Distribution Fund for the benefit of injured customers. This includes the $87,735,635 in civil penalties, which, under the Sarbanes-Oxley Act of 2002, may be distributed to victims in SEC enforcement actions. Without admitting or denying the charges, the firms also will consent to charges that they (a) willfully violated Exchange Act Section 11(b) and Rule 11b-1 by failing to maintain a fair and orderly market through their improper proprietary trading; (b) violated various NYSE rules; and (c) in certain interpositioning transactions involving six stocks at each firm, failed adequately to supervise certain of their individual specialists, who themselves engaged in fraud through that proprietary trading in violation of Exchange Act Section 10(b) and Rule 10b-5.

Barry W. Rashkover, Associate Director of the SEC's Northeast Regional Office, said, "This landmark settlement underscores the obligation of exchange specialists to serve public customer orders over the specialist's own proprietary interests. The settlement is excellent news for injured customers. Because of the Distribution Fund, they will be the ultimate beneficiaries of the firms' sizeable payments."

"This settlement reflects the culmination of a significant investigation and close cooperation between NYSE and the SEC," said David P. Doherty, executive vice president, NYSE Enforcement Division. "It sends a strong message that our individual and combined regulatory efforts are vigorous and demand nothing less than full compliance."

The NYSE and SEC found that the improper proprietary trading took various forms. Sometimes, certain of the firms' specialists "interpositioned" the firms' dealer accounts between customer orders by trading into both of them in succession – for example, buying into a customer market sell order first, and then selling, at a higher price, into the opposite market buy order, thus allowing the firm dealer account to profit from the spread. The regulators also found that the specialists traded for their dealer accounts ahead of executable agency orders on the same side of the market, orders that were executed later at prices inferior to the prices of dealer account trades. At other times, the specialists traded ahead of executable limit orders, which then went unexecuted and ultimately were canceled by the customers entering the orders.

The NYSE and SEC found that the interpositioning transactions, in particular, were heavily concentrated in a few stocks overseen by a small number of specialists at each firm. With certain interpositioning transactions in six stocks at each firm, the NYSE and SEC found that certain unnamed individual specialists engaged in fraud by violating their implied representations to public customers that they were limiting dealer transactions to those "reasonably necessary to maintain a fair and orderly market." None of the specialist firms, according to the findings, had in place reasonable systems or procedures to monitor, detect, or prevent those violations.

The investigation is continuing. The NYSE and SEC will continue to coordinate in the investigation of individual responsibility for the violative conduct that is the subject of the enforcement actions announced today.

(Attachment follows: "Payments in Settlement With Five NYSE Specialist Firms")

Payments in Settlement With Five NYSE Specialist Firms

Firm	Penalty	Disgorgement	Total
Bear Wagner Specialists LLC	$5,534,543	$10,724,903	**$16,259,446**
Fleet Specialist, Inc.	$21,083,875	$38,013,594	**$59,097,469**
LaBranche & Co., LLC	$21,872,320	$41,646,440	**$63,518,760**
Spear, Leeds & Kellogg Spec.	$16,496,406	$28,776,072	**$45,272,478**
Van der Moolen Specialists	$22,748,491	$34,926,613	**$57,675,104**
Total	$87,735,635	$154,087,622	**$241,823,257**

Exhibit 4: Scot Paltrow Writes

Scot Paltrow, a staff reporter of The Wall Street Journal, on December 23, 2002, writes the following key excerpts taken directly from his article. These are included here just to show that this whole affair is not just a concocted conspiracy theory by academic people. He states the following.

Why do Wall Street scandals recur with the grim regularity of earthquakes and forest fires? The obvious answer, of course, is that Wall Street is where the money is. Beyond the inevitable appeal of billions of dollars changing hands daily, however, lie more peculiar reasons why knavery on a grand scale periodically racks the securities industry.

Indeed, the language Wall Street traders and brokers use sometimes betrays disdain toward individual investors. Nasdaq market makers commonly refer to buy and sell orders from individuals as "dumb order flow," meaning their orders are almost certain to be profitable for the market makers because small investors typically trade without any hard information that could give them an advantage over these dealers.

One reason the risk of getting caught is small is that the securities industry's main regulator, the SEC, is overtaxed and chronically underfunded. Congress, under the influence of campaign contributions from Wall Street, consistently has resisted giving the SEC any sizable increase in funding.

When cases are brought, they invariably are settled. One result is that the penalties typically pale next to the amount of profits gained from the wrongdoing. Settlement numbers in the analysts' case seem large. But securities expert John C. Coffee Jr., a Columbia University law professor, contends they are only a small fraction of investors' losses from stocks that were excessively hyped by analysts.

Exhibit 5: Words by Glassman

James K. Glassman, the host of TechCentralStation.com, is presented here with some key excerpts from his article, dated May 4, 2003. As can be seen, the contents of this article, a portion of which is presented here, verify much of Ney's original philosophy from many years back.

On the SEC Probe of NYSE "Specialist" Firms: Time Free the Stock Market to Make it More Competitive

The real question is why the archaic system has lasted so long.

One reason is that the specialists are enormously powerful within the NYSE itself. The exchange became a non-profit corporation 30 years ago, with a 25-member board of directors. Representatives of three specialist firms - LaBranche & Co., Fleet Specialist, and Bear Wagner Specialists - sit on the board. The CEO of Bear Stearns Cos., which has a minority interest in Bear Wagner, is also on the board, as is the CEO of the Goldman Sachs Group, Inc., which owns a fourth specialist, Spear, Leads & Kellogg.

Another is that the NYSE operates as an exclusive club, with limited competition. Nearly all the trades in the stock of the largest U.S. companies, including 28 of the 30 Dow Jones Industrial Average, must occur on the floor of the NYSE. Companies that want to leave the exchange and move, say, to the NASDAQ, face severe restrictions from Rule 500, an infamous regulation of the exchange that critics liken to the code of the Cosa Nostra or a "Roach Motel": once you're in, you can't get out.

But more important than disclosure is competition. In a truly competitive market, companies don't last very long if they abuse the trust of customers. It's time to apply competitive market discipline to the world's largest stock market itself.

The problem is that the specialists play a dual role that is fraught with conflicts of interest.

Note: This article is in the context of the situation in the years before 2012.

Exhibit 6: Starbucks-Green Mountain Affair

This exhibit shows how the media can be used to manipulate prices and cause very heavy damage to stockholders. Things of this nature have not been studied very much, because these events go by unnoticed. In other words, it becomes part of the illusion where psychology is affected by consequences, but it is not perceived as such.

Here are the headlines from Reuters on March 8, 2012. Now, look at the words, "putting it in direct competition with partner Green Mountain....". When these headlines were released in the after-hours, GMCR plummeted.

By **Lisa Baertlein**
DETROIT | Thu Mar 8, 2012 10:13pm EST
(Reuters) - Starbucks Corp (SBUX.O) said it will launch its own single-cup coffee and espresso drink machine later this year, putting it in direct competition with partner Green Mountain Coffee Roasters Inc (GMCR.O), seller of the popular Keurig home brewers.

GMCR stock did nothing for days, but it did stay level as people continued to sell with someone buying (exchange insiders most likely). Someone big had to be buying, or the price would have fallen much more over those days. Then, on March 21, 2012, Starbucks released the following press release. Why did it take so long for this to occur? Now, consider the phrase that is used within the release. It says, "looking forward to working with our colleagues at GMCR to further accelerate growth in premium single-serve coffee." After so many GMCR stockholders took a beating of over ten points, it now seems that Starbucks and Green Mountain are sweet loving partners again. The point here is that the market makers were prepared for the initial press release. The press release was purposely formulated to cause stockholders to sell. Once that is done, the price will continue to go lower despite any corrective releases.

Of course, a miracle occurred. Once investors had unloaded their positions, there was a revelation released in the news. Once again, the CEO of Starbucks and the CEO of Green Mountain could not care less about its own stockholders that had sold on supposedly bad news.

Starbucks Press Release
Mar 21, 2012
Starbucks and Green Mountain Coffee Roasters, Inc. Expand Strategic Relationship

SEATTLE & WATERBURY, Vt., March 21, 2012 - Starbucks Coffee Company (NASDAQ: SBUX) and Green Mountain Coffee Roasters, Inc. (GMCR) (NASDAQ: GMCR), a leader in specialty coffee and coffee makers, today announced the expansion of their strategic relationship for the manufacturing, marketing, distribution and sale of Starbucksbranded Vue™ packs for use in GMCR's recently introduced Keurig® Vue™ Brewer.

"We are proud to expand our relationship with Green Mountain Coffee Roasters and are looking forward to working with our colleagues at GMCR to further accelerate growth in premium single-serve coffee," said Jeff Hansberry, president, Channel Development, for Starbucks. "Premium single cup is the fastest-growing segment of global coffee, and the expansion of our relationship with GMCR allows us to grow further, faster, in the single cup category."

Exhibit 7: Bureau of Labor Statistics

Current Population Survey (CPS)

There are about 60,000 households in the sample for this survey. This translates into approximately 110,000 individuals, a large sample compared to public opinion surveys which usually cover fewer than 2,000 people. The CPS sample is selected so as to be representative of the entire population of the United States. In order to select the sample, all of the counties and county-equivalent cities in the country first are grouped into 2,025 geographic areas (sampling units). The Census Bureau then designs and selects a sample consisting of 824 of these geographic areas to represent each State and the District of Columbia. The sample is a State-based design and reflects urban and rural areas, different types of industrial and farming areas, and the major geographic divisions of each State.

Every month, one-fourth of the households in the sample are changed, so that no household is interviewed more than 4 consecutive months. This practice avoids placing too heavy a burden on the households selected for the sample. After a household is interviewed for 4 consecutive months, it leaves the sample for 8 months, and then is again interviewed for the same 4 calendar months a year later, before leaving the sample for good. This procedure results in approximately 75 percent of the sample remaining the same from month to month and 50 percent from year to year.

Each month, 2,200 highly trained and experienced Census Bureau employees interview persons in the 60,000 sample households for information on the labor force activities (job holding and job seeking) or non-labor force status of the members of these households during the survey reference week (usually the week that includes the 12th of the month). At the time of the first enumeration of a household, the interviewer prepares a roster of the household members, including their personal characteristics (date of birth, sex, race, Hispanic ethnicity, marital status, educational attainment, veteran status, and so on) and their relationships to the person maintaining the household. This information, relating to all household members 15 years of age and over, is entered by the interviewers into laptop computers; at the end of each day's interviewing, the data collected are transmitted to the Census Bureau's central computer in Washington, D.C. (The labor force measures in the CPS pertain to individuals 16 years and over.) In addition, a portion of the sample is interviewed by phone through three central data collection facilities. (Prior to 1994, the interviews were conducted using a paper questionnaire that had to be mailed in by the interviewers each month.)

Each person is classified according to the activities he or she engaged in during the reference week. Then, the total numbers are "weighted," or adjusted to independent population estimates (based on updated decennial census results). The weighting takes into account the age, sex, race, Hispanic ethnicity, and State of residence of the person, so that these characteristics are reflected in the proper proportions in the final estimates.

A sample is not a total count, and the survey may not produce the same results that would be obtained from interviewing the entire population. But the chances are 90 out of 100 that the monthly estimate of unemployment from the sample is within about 290,000 of the figure obtainable from a total census. Since monthly unemployment totals have ranged between about 7 and 11 million in recent years, the possible error resulting from sampling is not large enough to distort the total unemployment picture.

Because these interviews are the basic source of data for total unemployment, information must be factual and correct. Respondents are never asked specifically if they are unemployed, nor are they given an opportunity to decide their own labor force status. Unless they already know how the Government defines unemployment, many of them may not be sure of their actual classification when the interview is completed.

Similarly, interviewers do not decide the respondents' labor force classification. They simply ask the questions in the prescribed way and record the answers. Based on information collected in the survey and definitions programmed into the computer, individuals are then classified as employed, unemployed, or not in the labor force.

All interviews must follow the same procedures to obtain comparable results. Because of the crucial role interviewers have in the household survey, a great amount of time and effort is spent maintaining the quality of their work. Interviewers are given intensive training, including classroom lectures, discussion, practice, observation, home-study materials, and on-the-job training. At least once a year, they attend day-long training and review sessions. Also, at least once a year, they are accompanied by a supervisor during a full day of interviewing to determine how well they carry out their assignments.

Reference from the Bureau of Labor Statistics

Exhibit 8: NYSE News Release

NYSE Regulation Fines Seven Specialist Firms $2.8 Million for Trading Violations

Specialist Firms Cited for Violations of Order Handling Obligations, Firm Quotes, Limit Order Displays, Short Sales and Intermarket Trading System Commitments

NEW YORK, January 16, 2007—NYSE Regulation, Inc. announced today it has censured and fined seven member organizations a total of $2.8 million for multiple trading violations, including failure to honor firm quote obligations. NYSE Regulation also censured and fined the seven specialist firms for their lack of written supervisory procedures relating to the firm quote rule.

"It is critically important for firms conducting business on the floor of the New York Stock Exchange to honor the publicly displayed price quotes in the course of buying and selling," said Susan Merrill, NYSE Regulation Chief of Enforcement. "These commitments are essential elements of the rules that govern trading and are codified in the NYSE Rules and federal securities regulations."

Under the firm quote rule, NYSE specialists are generally required to execute buy or sell orders that are presented to them at prices that are at least as favorable as the NYSE's published bid or offer at the time the orders enter the Exchange's electronic display book. On multiple occasions over a four-year period from 2003 through 2006, however, marketable orders did not receive the price of the published quote in effect at the time the order became viewable on the Exchange's electronic display book.

Similarly, the specialist firms failed to honor Intermarket Trading System (ITS) commitments to buy or sell. The ITS electronically links participating market centers and enables market professionals to interact with their counterparts in other markets whenever the nationwide Consolidated Quote System (CQS) shows a better price in another market. An ITS commitment to buy or sell must be priced at the offer or bid displayed by the market center to which the commitment is sent.

On multiple occasions during the relevant period, the specialist firms received ITS commitments from another market, yet the orders were not executed at the NYSE's published quotation before the commitment expired.

The specialist firms also failed to immediately display eligible limit orders, and improperly executed short sales on minus, or zero-minus ticks. Additionally, the firms lacked written supervisory procedures specifically relating to the Firm Quote

Rule during the period from January 2003 through August 2005. Bear Wagner Specialists LLC also failed to establish adequate written policies or procedures governing freezing of the Display Book.

The disciplinary actions against the seven member firms arose as a result of surveillances conducted by NYSE Regulation's Market Surveillance division and concern violations of Rule 11Ac1-1(c) under the Securities Exchange Act of 1934 (now designated as Rule 602(b) under Regulation NMS), and NYSE Rule 60, Rule 11Ac1-4 under the Securities Exchange Act of 1934 (now designated as Rule 604 under Regulation NMS), and NYSE Rule 79A.15, NYSE Rule 440B and Section 10(a) of the Securities Exchange Act of 1934 and Rule 10a-1(a) thereunder, and NYSE Rule 342.

The fines for the specialist firms are as follows (click on the firm name to access each individual Hearing Board Decision):

Spear, Leeds & Kellogg Specialists LLC	$600,000
LaBranche & Co. LLC	$600,000
Bear Wagner Specialists LLC	$550,000
Banc of America Specialists, Inc.	$500,000
Van der Moolen Specialists USA LLC	$400,000
Kellogg Specialist Group, LLC	$75,000
SIG Specialists, Inc.	$75,000
TOTAL:	$2,800,000

These violations occurred prior to the launch of Hybrid Market$_{SM}$ trading system enhancements that significantly limit the possibility of similar violations from occurring due to automatic execution and safeguards embedded into the Display Book.

In reaching these settlements, NYSE Regulation, Inc. took into consideration that the seven specialist firms assisted the NYSE by proposing enhancements and protective measures to the NYSE's systems and technology and that the activity described herein did not appear to have been undertaken with the intent to benefit the specialist firms. In agreeing to settle with NYSE Regulation, the specialist firms neither admitted nor denied the charges.

About NYSE Regulation
NYSE Regulation, Inc., is a not-for-profit corporation dedicated to strengthening market integrity and investor protection. It protects investors by regulating the activities of member organizations through the enforcement of marketplace rules and federal securities laws. NYSE member organizations hold 98 million customer accounts or 84 percent of the total public customer accounts handled by broker-

dealers. Total assets of NYSE member organizations are over $4 trillion. They operate from 20,000 branch offices around the world and employ 195,000 registered personnel. NYSE Regulation, Inc. also ensures that companies listed on the NYSE and on NYSE Arca meet their financial and corporate governance listing standards.

NYSE Regulation consists of four divisions: Market Surveillance, Member Firm Regulation, Enforcement and Listed Company Compliance, as well as a Risk Assessment unit and Dispute Resolution/Arbitration. For more information, visit our website at www.nyseregulation.com .

****

The following reference is by Paul Barnes. As the reader can see, there are others out there that agree with the conclusions of "Legally Crooked." This is not a conspiracy theory.

We should not be fooled into believing that the existence of a vast amount of law and regulations is evidence of protection. On the contrary, it is more likely to suggest the difficulty of the regulators in policing it. The best protection for investors is the scepticism of the press and the market. The maxim 'A fool and his money are soon parted' applies. I have argued that the market is regarded as 'efficient' because it is rational. It is perhaps a more apt to say that its scepticism makes it efficient. Commentators freely believe the market is open to abuse and, whilst it may not be rife, insider dealing is common. Whilst this continues to be said and disbelief about the effectiveness of the control in financial intermediaries remains, there will be both pressure for, and scope for, improvement.

Reference:
Barnes, Paul. Stock Market Efficiency, Insider Dealing and Market Abuse. Farnham, Surrey, GBR: Ashgate Publishing Group, 2009. p 16. http://site.ebrary.com/lib/ncent/Doc?id=10362150&ppg=215

Anthony Campos

"Whenever I commit an error in judgment, I read my own book, and lo and behold; I always find that I did not follow my own word."

Tony Campos, PhD revised photo 2018

From the idealistic beginnings of the academic world to the real-world awakening of the Vietnam conflict, this person has witnessed human nature in many forms. His jobs through life have included jewelry worker, factory assembler, textile worker, armored truck driver, security officer, salesman, Navy Sea Bee, photographer, Bank of America loan officer, publisher, stockbroker, driving instructor, driving school owner, and college instructor. His stock market newsletter commentary began in August of 1983. He passed the series 7 broker's license examination in 1988.

He was born on April 30, 1943, in Pawtucket, Rhode Island. He graduated from Tolman High School in Pawtucket, Rhode Island in June of 1962. He later graduated from the University of California at Santa Barbara with a BA in economics and then received an MBA in business management from Golden Gate University. He now holds an accredited PhD from Northcentral University with a specialization in electronic commerce.

Tribute to the Average Investor

My inclination in life is to drive the human mind toward logic and reasoning in the battle against deception. This battle can only be won if people better understand human nature and human motivations for any event or situation that may be encountered. My ambition in life has always been to present and to perform something unusual. That is why I created this book.

Thank you for looking at my work.

Sincerely,

Anthony Campos

205